CAMBRIDGE STUDIES IN AMERICAN LITERATURE
AND CULTURE

Sublime Enjoyment

Linking classic American literature to contemporary popular culture, *Sublime Enjoyment* argues that the rational systems of normal social life are motivated and sustained by "perverse" desires. This perversity arises from the failure of symbolic satisfactions – love, work, success – to make us happy, and from our refusal to accept that failure. Hoping to achieve satisfaction, we respond ultimately to situations that evoke older, more primary drives and their attendant emotions. But while a conventional pervert knows exactly what to want, the healthy pervert must find enjoyment inadvertently: in the abject of the sublime, in duty and reason, and in the obligations of a "fun morality." Examining the ways in which this inadvertence is represented in American literature and culture, Dennis Foster identifies ways that longings are linked to social forces.

D1544428

Books in the series

Continued on pages following the index

SUBLIME ENJOYMENT

On the Perverse Motive
in American Literature

DENNIS A. FOSTER

Southern Methodist University

CAMBRIDGE
UNIVERSITY PRESS

PUBLISHED BY THE PRESS SYNDICATE OF THE UNIVERSITY OF CAMBRIDGE
The Pitt Building, Trumpington Street, Cambridge CB2 1RP, United Kingdom

CAMBRIDGE UNIVERSITY PRESS
The Edinburgh Building, Cambridge CB2 2RU, United Kingdom
40 West 20th Street, New York, NY 10011–4211, USA
10 Stamford Road, Oakleigh, Melbourne 3166, Australia

First published 1997

Printed in the United States of America

Typeset in Baskerville

Library of Congress Cataloging-in-Publication Data
Foster, Dennis A.
Sublime enjoyment : on the perverse motive in American literature
/ Dennis A. Foster.
p. cm. – (Cambridge studies in American literature and
culture)
Includes bibliographical references (p.   ).
ISBN 0-521-58437-x
1. American literature – History and criticism.   2. Sublime, The,
in literature.   3. Pleasure in literature.   4. Popular culture –
United States.   5. Desire in literature.   6. Literature and
society – United States – History.   7. National characteristics,
American, in literature.   8. Aesthetics, American.
9. Psychoanalysis and literature – United States.   10. American
literature – Psychological aspects.   I. Title.   II. Series.
PS169.S84F67   1997
810.9'353 – dc21   96-40352
                                                                CIP

*A catalogue record for this book is available from
the British Library.*

ISBN 0 521 58437 x hardback

CONTENTS

v

ACKNOWLEDGMENTS

I cannot say when this book first began to be written, but *perversion* started to organize my writing following a discussion of the concept at the first Lacan Seminar in English. The open, generous conversation of the seminar's participants during those four weeks initiated a turn of thought that gradually centered the work I had been doing. Very gradually. As I complained to John Paul Riquelme, my chair at the time, that my leave was flying by while I was stuck attempting an introduction, he wisely advised me to abandon it and write, instead, what turned out to be the chapter on J. G. Ballard, where I discovered what the book was really about. And long after I should have been turning the screw on this topic one last time, I heard from a third party that John Carlos Rowe had told someone I was working on "the sublime," and half of my book fell into place. The dropped word, the incidental advice, the joke, and other such accidents that arose from my interactions with friends and colleagues have laid on me debts that most of them would not know they were owed.

There are others who have more directly and consistently played roles in the development of my thought. For years, a reading group at SMU has led me through the texts of Freud and revealed the richness and oddity of his writing. Steven V. Daniels, Ann and Robert Hunter, Beth Newman, and Nina Schwartz – the stalwarts of the group – left me time after time with insights that I carried directly back to my desk. Philip Kuberski's inventive, prolific conversation has so thoroughly infused my way of thinking that I sometimes wonder if I have ever had a thought of my own. His prompt and unselfish reading of the typescript at a point when I could hardly bear to continue enabled me to imagine for the first time that my pages were a book. My sister Betsy has warned me for years that I had better write this book so that she could read it, and that injunction has haunted every line I revised. But the most profound debt must go to Nina Schwartz, who has probably read the typescript more often than I have and showed me how to improve every page. During discussions with her, the clarity of her mind repeatedly illuminated my thesis when I worked myself into a dark confusion. I cannot imagine having completed this book without her help.

Because books also require material assistance to be written, I need to acknowledge the research leave SMU granted me in 1994–5, which gave me the time I needed to write the second half of the book. The external and internal readers for Cambridge University Press commented with wonderful thoroughness and insight on the typescript and helped me clarify numerous elements of my argument. In addition, I would like to thank the following institutions for granting permission to include versions of previously published essays: Oxford University Press for "Pleasure and Community in Cultural Criticism," *ALH* (1994): 371–82; the Arizona Board of Regents for "Re-Poe Man: A Problem of Pleasure," *Arizona Quarterly* 4 (1990): 1–26; Duke University Press for "Alphabetic Pleasures: *The Names*," *SAQ* (1990): 395–412; and the Modern Language Association of America for "J. G. Ballard's Empire of the Senses: Perversion and the Failure of Authority," *PMLA* (1993): 519–32.

1

INTRODUCTION

THE PROBLEM WITH PLEASURE

Too much or too little. Hysterics come too late, always certain that this is not the one; obsessives come too soon, afraid of missing their chance (Samuels). There is always a problem with pleasure, and not just among the unhealthy, depressed, or neurotic. It is easy to find oneself leaping too quickly or hesitating for too long. Even those of us who put off our own pleasure for the good of our children, God, country, or other causes – and who therefore can feel good about renouncing overt satisfaction – usually remain convinced that others are getting more than their fair share: as the Lacanian critic Slavoj Žižek puts it, we suppose someone is enjoying himself, and we do not like it.[1] And yet, this subject whom we suppose to be enjoying himself helps us to make sense of our own lack of happiness by attributing knowledge and enjoyment to some enviable but distasteful other whose music is too loud and food too smelly. Only perverts and children seem actually to enjoy themselves, a state of affairs that most healthy citizens recognize and that discourages us from a too vigorous pursuit of pleasure, a pursuit few would know how to conduct in any case.

The proper systems for pleasure – sex, violence, looking, food – work intermittently and poorly, which is probably a good thing. For to compensate for what we seem to be missing, we work, raise families, strive: we make civilization. And yet, it seems unlikely that something as complex as human culture could be sustained by rewards as diffuse as money, public admiration, unruly children. Ultimately, I suspect, we respond to older, more primary drives or, rather, to situations that recall those older drives and their attendant emotions, whether of joy or horror. In this book I am asking how such a capacity for elementary enjoyment could be linked to social forces. Let me begin with Oedipus.

Perhaps, as Jocasta explains, boys do dream of killing their fathers and marrying their mothers.[2] But this wish would not get at the heart of the oedipal fantasy. Certainly, something unconscious is at work in Oedipus' rage and desire when he kills Laius and becomes king; otherwise he would not be so horrified to discover at the play's end that he is the criminal. However, Oedipus does not have to look inward to find himself moved toward parricide and incest: it was the Oracle who had said he would commit these crimes. Something beyond Oedipus' desires, beyond his individual motives, drives him to act despite his determination not to do so. The question, then, for Sophocles, would be how he could manage to have Oedipus fulfill his required fate without arousing Oedipus' own horror at such actions. Oedipus could not simply go to his father and kill him, even if he knew who he was. Rather, he does the prudent and honorable thing and leaves his home, a course that frees him to slay older men and sleep with older women to his heart's content, which he does, each time because it is the right thing to do. Had Laius and Jocasta not been his actual parents, he might, at worst, be faulted for covertly fulfilling a secret impulse by redirecting the aim of his desire – he sleeps with *this* older woman, the queen, instead of *that* older woman, Mother. Or perhaps that is the *best* we could say for him, given that the ready alternative – that he kills and marries out of a pure sense of duty and honor – speaks badly for duty and honor.

Too little capacity for pleasure in people with power frightens reasonable people, because we know that lacking pleasure, those with power find other, scarier enjoyments[3]: the conquest of nations, the beating of wives and children. In the case of Oedipus, the possibilities for pleasure opened to him by the Oracle's promise are too monstrous for him to accept: by pointing to what he cannot have, the prediction effectively leads him to understand that what he wants is impossible, and he may as well renounce his desire. But renunciation opens another path to him, that of submission. Rather than pursue his own pleasure, he can become the tool of the Oracle, of the gods, deriving his enjoyment from submitting to the will of a greater power, fate. And so he adheres to the law, striking down the old man who would dishonor him at the crossroads, marrying the queen for the good of a grateful people. And if it is the gods' desire that through his obedience he gain the impossible enjoyments of parricide and incest, at least he was not moved by his *own* desire, at least his actions were ethical.

In the story of Oedipus, one of the inaugural moments of Western culture, we find the social good bound to an ancient and exterior drive, to a fate that precedes and remains exterior to the individual person. Thebes is relieved of both the Sphinx's oppression and the apparently infertile (and hence politically destabilizing) king, and Oedipus is able to enact a drama that might never have occurred to him had it not been whispered to him by the Oracle. That is, the social order of Thebes seems to enlist Oedipus to do its work by providing a means for him to act out perverse, unconscious, and ultimately disastrous desires that he might otherwise have renounced or remained ignorant of. Like Oedipus, we fulfill our fates because our motives remain unknown to us. When Freud called perversion the opposite of neurosis (1905), he meant that the pervert finds a way to enjoy what the neurotic must repress, to pursue what he wants while the normal neurotic turns away. For each of us there is a point at which satisfaction is impossible and not just forbidden: at first we are too young, too weak to get what we think we want, and later we find that the pleasure we seek is not finally the pleasure we wanted, that something is always still missing. It is as if a piece of nature, as Freud puts it, has decreed from the start that the thing we most desire will be lost. Faced with these limits, the pervert looks around for an escape, for some way to evade this fate. The pervert *denies* the laws of nature and culture that limit enjoyment, laws that Freud refers to under the term "castration." He finds a stage on which the drama of desire can be played out, replaying an enjoyment in spite of all boundaries, while for the normal, more or less neurotic person, castration is accepted, the real loss forgotten. But the law of social life that limits desire also implants its perverse opposite, burying that opposite within the very structures that are supposed to keep the destructive drives at bay. The healthy, that is, can still find their enjoyment, perverse or sublime, through the exercise of law.

3

Why did Freud call the child's sublime openness to pleasure "polymorphous perversity" if not as a defensive rejection of his own discovery (1905: 191)? The boldness of this formulation is that it locates the wellspring of humankind's wild variety of sexual pleasures in the natural richness of the infant body. It is a Wordsworthian moment to see the child as father of the man in sexuality above all. With one exception, all subsequent forms of sexuality are disdained as perverse fixations on a prior state, as if adult perversity were merely a degenerate remainder of the original pleasure some seducer teased from a responsive child. Only the "normal" sexuality of the genitally, heterosexually organized adult escapes being condemned as perversion. The proof of this escape is that healthy, genital (and male) sex provides such modest pleasure: Freud writes with something like wonder of the lingering taste for perverse pleasures in "uncultivated women" and prostitutes, as well as in all those many other women (by which he must mean otherwise decent wives, sisters, and mothers) with "an aptitude for prostitution" who have, by sheer good or bad fortune, not plied the trade. And yet, normal sexuality, with its various disgusts and shame, provides a haven for that infant body, as a witness protection program preserves the knowledge of the crime by giving the witness a new name and occupation.

When Freud turned to the problem of destruction in *Civilization and Its Discontents*, his principal concern was with the consequences of civilization's having driven aggressive drives into an unconscious, and therefore unreasoning, space where they might flourish without restraint. In his relentless dualism, Freud insisted on separating sex and death drives and therefore found that deprived of uninhibited sexuality, we grow sad; deprived of uninhibited violence, we grow guilty. But as this text shows in an exemplary fashion, Freud's attempt to hold to this dualism leads him into endless revisions and complications throughout the essay as love and death twist together: the pleasure principle falls under the death drive while life is sustained only by the violence of renewal. The apparent confusions may be ultimately rhetorical: Freud wanted to find that the impediment to a peaceful world was an internal tendency toward aggression, that the ancient nemesis was Death. A good man, Freud wanted to choose life. But in his clearest articulation of the death drive, he defined it as a tendency to return to the inanimate, to the most peaceful state possible. Which leaves Life as the problem.

Throughout this book I will be following this line of argument in a principally American context, looking at the ways that abject, perverse longings are appropriated to serve socially useful ends. We become, for example, Americans in the service of demands that appeal to ancient longings within us, but which care nothing for our personal good. The songs, pledges, and images that American children learn from near-infancy help to instill a sense of sublime nationalism that transcends any rational commitment to whatever principles might constitute an American character, leading people to declare their Americanness even when their values are deeply at odds with the country's constitution, laws, and social traditions. It is a compulsive repetition of the practices of America, not a reasoned appreciation of the benefit (or harm) that might derive from a commitment to the state, that makes us who we are. The perverse that runs through normal, healthy society comes from a deep unwillingness to accept symbolic satisfactions – love, work, success – as sufficient for happiness because they contain obscure, disturbing traces of an impossible enjoyment. In one way or another, we will seek to repair this loss, but while a proper pervert knows what he wants, the healthy pervert must find enjoyment inadvertently: in the abject or the sublime, in duty and reason, in the obligations of a "fun morality." My task in this book is to examine the ways in which this inadvertence is exploited by cultural forms for their own ends.

The following chapters explore various crossings between the sublime and the perverse in order to analyze motivations in modern, mostly American, culture. I focus on America because it has been, from its first European explorations, a space of fantasy, sublime in its sheer distance and scale. But it has been perverse as well in the ways merchants, explorers, and the various misfits who came to this land denied the limitations that the laws of God, king, and nature had imposed on them. Whether people came looking for God or gold, they came hoping to restore the losses that haunted their old world, to make something whole out of the new. We see in Americans a continual capacity to be surprised by and disappointed in the failure of their various communities – schools, churches, workplaces, governments – to produce a clear and open space in which to engage with others, as if simple greed or stupidity were to blame. The desires that move us are older and less human than we know.

In my next chapter I take up that hope as it is expressed in a desire for "community," for a social, religious, or economic organization that works, beginning with the phenomenon of Berkeley in the 1960s. The persistence of the hope expressed by that movement, coupled with an equally engrained cynicism, leads me to attempt to work through what we mean by the words "community" and "human." The work of Lyotard and Nancy, here, helps me to conceive of alternative relations to others and society, relations that acknowledge the fundamental impediments to human interactions, the "unworking" nature of social existence. What both writers express is the profoundly individual nature of enjoyment, even when it is achieved through social interaction. Community does not "work," although it provides forms that allow us to find compensation for the unavoidable necessity of dwelling with others. The question I ask concerns the importance, if any, of recognizing the perversity in this compensation.

The chapters on Poe and James that follow pick up the idea of the archaic heart that inhabits the new world. For Poe, as for Hawthorne, America has always been old: the old men are oppressive, the houses are ancient, and bodies are buried everywhere. The theory of the cosmos Poe develops in *Eureka* points to the compulsion to repeat that drives all life: the grave is the origin as well as the premature end in Poe's world. And it is the attraction to this past that he sees as the perverse double to American optimism, infusing every part of social, economic, as well as personal life. In the world James inhabits, this compulsion to dig up the past has been woven into the moral and aesthetic fantasies of American life. The publishing scoundrel of "The Aspern Papers" has so thoroughly romanticized his obsession with a lost, sublime past that he remains oblivious to his more abject, morbid interests in the parental body of the great, dead Aspern. But Juliana Bordereau, like Madame de Vionnet in *The Ambassadors,* has little trouble seeing the connection between the American's obsession and the cultural enterprise of commerce. The women see that American money, in particular, moves with the

6

liquid flux of enjoyment, and they exploit it. This connection, in fact, is the great lesson that Madame de Vionnet teaches young Chad, the very image of advertising and manliness, who is returning to America to tap the money flowing through a dawning consumer culture.

The lesson is both well learned and easily forgotten. When De-Lillo looks at Americans abroad in *The Names,* most of them are still obsessed with the fantasy that they can touch a sublime reality, one that lies in the rock of archeological digs or in the "abecedarian" immediacy of words and letters scratched in ancient stone. But the characters' fixations on an irrecoverable loss make them the fool of anyone who would use them. It is as if the very capacity for love, commitment, and passion, insofar as it is rooted in that distant memory of wholeness, can make these expatriates effective agents of the CIA, make them exporters of an American vision that is at least as cultural as economic or political. In many of his books, the British novelist J. G. Ballard looks at this American culture with an appalled fascination. He points to the ways post–World War II America displaced earlier notions of sublimity around the world with those generated by technology, particularly in its production of cars and film. The meanings of freedom, sexuality, individuality, and life itself have come to be defined by the automobile, the magazine image, the film event. They stage the fantasy of enjoyment, the traumatic loss that lies at the core of every human. And Ballard sees in the world's embracing of these fantasies the fetishism of cars, terrorism, violence, and other disturbing yet typical behaviors of his era.

William S. Burroughs, the modern master of the American perverse, produces a history of the world in *Cities of the Red Night* (1981) that attempts to account for the failure of the West to produce the freedom that might have been possible. He tells a story of the pirate Captain Mission's attempt to found a society that would not be based on repression, greed, and violence. What he reveals is that suffering is not simply a consequence of oppression. Rather, the relation between freedom and slavery depends on how enjoyment is distributed: too often, enjoyment and slavery are allied. The history of the West, Burroughs seems to suggest, is the history of how enjoyment has been appropriated. America is the end of a historical development that contains in its failures the traces of a past he cannot bear to give up, one to which we will continue to return.

Death: The Problem Drive

The 1986 film *The Hitcher* opens with a boy enacting the death drive in classic Freudian terms: he is falling asleep at the wheel. Hoping for some relief from the drive, he picks up a hitcher, a psychotic killer played by Rutger Hauer, who soon offers, literally, to kill the boy. The offer induces a trancelike state in which the driver nearly asks for death but at the last second screams "No!" and forces the hitcher from the car. The rest of the movie falls into two sections: in the first, the killer pursues the boy, who is now eager to stay alive, even though his desire seems to result in the deaths of all who come near him. In the second half, the film turns, and we realize that the hitcher's role has become to save the boy, not just from himself but from the now murderously angry police who are chasing him, thinking him the killer. The boy can, in the end, live only by killing the hitcher, by becoming more like him, an ironic, brutal figure of Life. A good movie.

B-movies, like Jim Thompson novels, often provide startlingly direct insights into our passionate lives. What I find clarifying in this movie is that it links life not to pleasure, but to maintaining some intensity, irrespective of its horror or pleasure. This intensity is not Nietzsche's Will to Power, although such a force could be one form it takes. Violence, that is, is not the only form in which a vital drive toward intense life might appear, but it happens that way often enough to make me doubt the separation of a death drive from a drive toward life or eros. Insofar as the death drive functions as a *return* to a prior state, it has, I think, nothing to do with being dead. Rather, it represents an obsessive return to a traumatic opening where the subject recoiled from an encounter with an impossible Real. In a pattern of approach and avoidance that Lacan describes as *"tuché and automaton"* (1978: 53ff), the subject returns like an automaton *"as if by chance"* (54) to the moment of a traumatic encounter: "Is it not remarkable that, at the origin of the analytic experience, the real should have presented itself in the form of that which is *unassimilable* in it – in the form of the trauma, determining all that follows, and imposing on it an apparently accidental origin?" (55). This encounter remains a "missed encounter," the compelling yet mysterious event that marks a being for life, and for death, shattering the image of simple fullness that had defined life's purpose prior to the traumatic, incomprehensible event.

The path of intensity first draws infants away from the original, unformed satisfaction of the newly born. At birth, thriving is not the only choice. Like Nathanael West's desperate lonelyhearts, many newborns are moved only by violence, warmed only by friction until they have been taught appetite: to hunger, to suck. Our weak human instincts need to be supplemented by training, given a taste for intensity that will keep us from returning to the abyss of sleep. Once taught the trick of living, the individual creature returns to this scene of instruction, seeking to repeat the trick in the face of temptations to succumb to a drowsy death. The boy in the car is willing simply to fall asleep and die until the hitcher offers to assist. If there is a dualism here, then, it is between intensity and sleep, "enjoyment" and pleasure. That is, eros and thanatos, despite the different emotions evoked by them, are equally capable of serving the drive toward enjoyment. Only when the subject has once achieved a place in symbolic culture can enjoyment be bent to moral purposes, to forms of pleasure that draw differences between eros and death. But even then, enjoyment persists as an underlying, sustaining force in erotic and aggressive drives, as well as their more civil sublimations, driving us forward, despite their failures to provide full satisfaction.

A death drive, I am arguing, is the reasonable mind's interpretation of a movement toward something like a Lacanian Real, toward that other, unrepresentable world that sustains our symbolically lived world: it moves toward the sublime. In that other world, "I" is both dead and not yet alive, and *I* return to it as invariably as any zombie to his master. The revulsion we often feel about the death drive is not in its leading us to the famous inanimate state, the place of no desire, of sleep or annihilation, but its absolute denial of the subject's will and control.

Another example: in the 1989 film *Dead Calm,* the woman Rae drives her baby through a rainy night singing "The Itsy Bitsy Spider."

9

She crashes and the baby dies. She subsequently fails to thrive, as they say of certain neonates, and her husband takes her on a hot, empty cruise to recover. The dead calm of their boat matches that of her depressed, sedated state: she strives for the inertial stillness of Freud's death drive. Her recovery begins when her child "returns," not as an infant, but as Billy Zane, a two-year-old in an adult body whose only interests are sex and destruction.[4] He tries to kill her husband, rapes her, and yet still looks at her with a baby's open and wondering eyes. Only when she can look into those eyes and reject him can she return to the symbolic world: she "finds" what she has "lost," but it is her husband, now, not her baby – the phallus (who actually kills the "baby"), not the baby-fetish. The spider is washed down the spout into the sewers, the bowels of the house, only to reemerge into the light. This film recognizes that the spider is not simply the evil that returns to haunt our existence, but an image of life's dependence on regular messages from the drain.

The Real Sublime

The triumph of the Enlightenment in the modern world depended absolutely on the ascendancy of symbolic representation as the condition of knowledge. When Descartes divided the world into the inner and the outer, the mental and the physical, the knowable and the unknowable, he laid the foundations for a scientific capture of the world. Knowledge of what lay outside the mind – the entire material, measurable, universe – was given over to a mode of representation governed by empirical observation. The age of science that followed came to define knowledge as such in terms of its own representational system and insisted on the priority of its terms in all questions of reality. Although Descartes held questions of spirit, imagination, and transcendence to belong to another, and ultimately more significant, realm of knowledge, when he set aside this higher "truth" of the material world as unrepresentable, it became an untouchable realm. Philosophy, following the path of certainty initiated by the "I think," would take this sublime realm as its own proper field, but in doing so remove it from our daily lives. Consequently, as Descartes argues, the authority of church and king lay beyond pragmatic questioning, and their laws remain (until the ultimate questions are resolved by philosophy) unchallenged.[5] Descartes did not destroy but ultimately preserved the unrepresentable from the penetration of science, just as he preserved the authority of the divinely ordained monarch from the challenge of the individual subject. Ever since, the project of emancipation – the history of the rational individual's liberation – has been in conflict with the preserve of faith, where a people rely on an originating, unknowable power for its own power and authority.[6]

It was Kant, however, who in his attempt to finalize matters (as always) opened up the most troubling dimension of this conflict. In defining what Burke and others had really meant by the "sublime," Kant identified an effect produced when some event permits one to conceive of what cannot be represented: "to think the unattainability of nature regarded as the presentation of ideas" (134). The sublime leads one, that is, to imagine a Real that cannot be grasped, a reality "not pre-adapted to our judgment" (103). The unknowable attracts us, but its resistance to the mind's grasp makes it both threatening and repellent (102): "The transcendent . . . is for the Imagination like an abyss in which it fears to lose itself" (120). The strong emotion produced in the sublime experience derives from its giving us access to such transcendental ideas that, in their resistance to being represented, provide the basis for representation. The sublime event, that is, suggests what is both prior to and beyond the representable. But whether that basis, that prior, realm is ultimately the guarantee of representation's validity (a real beyond appearance) or a formless horror against which the representation is a defense cannot be determined. That which was placed safely outside of consideration by Descartes has reemerged as horrifying and tempting for Kant. A man of faith, Kant had to see that unconditioned, incomprehensibly real noumenal world as an aspect of the divine. But clearly, the emotional intensity of the encounter adds to the sublime's appeal: in the face of the sublime, a "momentary checking of the vital powers" is followed by a "consequent stronger outflow of them" (102). The sublime, which derives from both cultural and inborn factors (130–1), provides an intensity that is both dangerous and necessary to life. The lure of the sublime, that is, arises where reason and representation fail to provide in themselves a needed enjoyment and knowledge.

By emphasizing Kant's formulation of the sublime as I have, I have allied it with the Lacanian Real, another realm of the unrepresentable. This Real also has the ambiguous quality of being both prior to and a consequence of symbolic forms. The Real does not encompass the entire unsymbolized universe, though it touches the realm of inhuman existence. The Real, as Žižek points out, is evoked by the implicit limits of symbolic representation, by the fact that something is always excluded: the limit creates the beyond, the prior, the silence.[7] The triumph of the Symbolic brings with it its own mad other, its failure, its realm of freedom. But the crucial point here is that the Real is not a general or universal reality, the same everywhere for all people; rather, it is evoked by the particular qualities in the forms of symbolic representation at work for a given subject. This is why it can at times take the form of the sublime, at other times that of the abject.

The concept of the Real forms the dynamic heart of Lacan's later work. The Real is the place to which we always return, the stumbling block, the unresolved encounter, the impossible: these are among the many phrases Lacan uses to describe its place and function. The Real names some stain, an obscurity in every representation that remains fascinating without ever rising to the level of becoming an object of desire. It is what can be neither understood nor ignored and therefore is never a source of satisfaction. Given sufficient scale, the Real might resemble traditional examples of the sublime: the mountain, the storm, the sea. In the midst of these magnitudes, you can never see everything, and those things that escape you suggest a power you cannot properly imagine. On more intimate levels, the Real takes on qualities of the abject: the scar, the obscure pain, the gut feeling, and other shadows we probe and ponder. But whether or not any specific event produces the sensation of the Real depends on the ways in which one's connection to the symbolic network has been formed. In every case, the Real refers to that property of experience that prevents any rational project from reaching completion, that precludes any representation of the world from being fully adequate to one's experience of it.

Sublime Bolo Bolo

In 1985, Semiotext(e) published a small book entitled *Bolo'Bolo*. The writer, P.M., looks at a world dominated by what he calls the Planetary Work-Machine, a system of compulsive labor and war that dominates all space and activity, keeping us all busy (even those with no jobs) and anxiety-ridden. P.M. argues that the human project that began several thousand years ago with the discovery of agriculture has in the past two hundred years threatened to degrade the air, land, and seas and to overpopulate all human habitats; at the same time, we contemplate a nuclear abortion to the project. What had seemed to be a guarantee of increasing wealth has become a machine that proceeds out of its own internal compulsions. P.M.'s "solution" is Bolo'Bolo, a network of small, mostly self-sufficient communities where basic economic needs can be met while at the same time both primitive (tribal, genetic) needs and modern obsessions can be satisfied. What I find compelling in this book, half-joke though it may be, is the suggestion that some kind of primary human need, something that served the species well for hundreds of thousands of years, has been appropriated by a cultural system, the work-machine. Because our fundamental capacity for enjoyment finds expression through the "machine," one will never be able to change this system simply by pointing out to people that their interests are not being served by their "work." Before change is possible, that is, we need to recognize how we get our enjoyment, to see that the primitive body has been connected to the cultural project, linking enjoyment to productivity and reason.

Psychoanalysis has conventionally conceived of the relationship between drive and civilization to involve the repression and displacement of drives, which results in frustration and a loss of pleasure. Within the system of repression, for example, the symptom represents the reemergence of the drive in a manner that makes the subject ill. The cure for this illness, then, is to understand through anamnesis (the work of remembering and working through) the desire that sustains the symptom and, by maturely accepting the loss of pleasure and the attending sadness, dissolve the symptom and get on with life. Freud's failure to cure the Wolf Man, however, gave Abraham and Torok a clue to another mechanism at work in the symptom: cryptonymy, the magic word. They concluded that the ultimate effect of the Wolf Man's analysis was not to dissolve the symptom but to preserve within the language of analysis another hidden source of enjoyment that could be silently visited through the therapeutic sessions. The Wolf Man thereby exploited Freud and his other analysts' procedures to both sustain and conceal his secret practice, from himself as well as from them.

The idea that our sense of being is built up around an unspoken and indissoluble core appears in Lacan's later writings as the "sinthome," a play on "symptom" that calls up associations with sin, saint, Saint Thomas, synthetic man (*homme*). The word refers not to a classical symptom but to the fantasy that founds the subject, to some moment of arrested enjoyment to which he or she will always return. Because the sinthome is so basic, the kernel of the subject, there is ultimately no possibility of dissolving it. The ends of psychoanalysis, consequently, do not take one past the fantasy, but through it, to a point where one can accept one's sinthome as one's own. This conclusion suggests that one finds the deepest satisfaction in something unconnected to the world of health and reason. In the formulation Lacan reached in the essay on the Mirror Stage, he writes that psychoanalysis should "accompany the patient to the ecstatic limit of the '*Thou art that.*'" In quoting from the *Upanishads,* evoking the nothing from which the subject arises, Lacan suggests the sublime ends of the practice that the sinthome ultimately names.

Just as the concepts of the "magic word" and the "sinthome" arise to take account of a core of enjoyment in the subject, *Bolo'Bolo* proposes a society organized around the preservation of enjoyment: "In a larger city we could find the following *bolos:* Alco-bolo, Symbolo, Sado-bolo, Maso-bolo, Vegi-bolo, Les-bolo, Franko-bolo, Italo-bolo, Play-bolo, No-bolo . . ." (80). The suggestion here is that each of us would be able to claim our particular core of enjoyment and live according to its dictates. The realization of this project is unlikely, of course, but P.M. presents this list as a strategy for "substructing" the Planetary Work-Machine. That is, rather than encourage open rebellion or covert subversion of the dominant system, he points to the real power of culture – its promise of obscure enjoyment – which he hopes could be undone by building an alternative

14

practice beneath it. By staging a perversion, each bolo at the very least lets its community acknowledge that the real sources of enjoyment are not in the rational goals of society, and that enjoyment might be achieved with less destruction of self and world if the sustaining fantasy were embraced.

The problem with P.M.'s plan, of course, is that the Planetary Work-Machine is already Sublime-bolo: the businesses of work and war have found ways of promising enjoyment or, rather, of denying its impossibility. And here I introduce my central argument for this book: for the past century, since the discovery of consumption as a meaningful occupation for life, culture has increasingly been sustained by perverse drives. Baudrillard, for example, in "Consumer Society" refers to the "fun morality" (1988: 48) of consumption. This recently invented labor has shifted the location of "fun" from a personal pursuit of satisfaction to an obligation to a higher principle: one submits to fun not for its immediate delights but for the perverse enjoyments of duty. Such duties are the sign of what I am calling Sublime-bolo concealed within the Work-Machine.

Cultures and religions that had for centuries functioned through repression – which means that people accepted the idea that only god and king had the might and right to enjoy themselves – have begun to operate on the denial of the loss of pleasure. This denial appears, for example, in the turn that religions – particularly those that constitute what Harold Bloom calls the American Religion – have taken toward fundamentalisms with their claims of a fully comprehensible gospel, glossolalia, and cash rewards. For Bloom, the essence of the American Religion is the conviction of knowing (gnosticism): "Their deepest knowledge is that they were no part of Creation, but existed as spirits before it, and so are as old as God himself" (57). No knowledge is beyond recapture, no enjoyment ultimately impossible. The risen Christ teaches the faithful even of the death he has mastered. God, that is, does not function in these religious practices as a promise of eventual enjoyment and as compensation for its absence in this world; rather, God serves to deny the suggestion that you do not deserve to be requited for your suffering now. The significant point here is that the unintentionally perverse enjoyment at the heart of such religions has the effect of

15

sustaining, for example, capitalism, which is never based simply on an economic model of wealth but depends as well on the pressure to enjoy.

Consciousness

One of the more peculiar, if symptomatic, projects of contemporary philosophy involves the attempts to describe the mind in terms of a computer. For example, Daniel Dennett's massive *Consciousness Explained* is an extraordinary attempt to demystify the "Cartesian theater" model of consciousness, the notion that some center of consciousness rules our brains, not only by demonstrating that this model does not work (which he does convincingly) but also by proposing a fantastically complex computer as a model of the brain's function and production of consciousness. Dennett wants to remove the mystery of consciousness, mostly because it leads people to mystify thought and, consequently, makes them unable to think logically. He clings to the notion of a machine mind but, in calling it the Joyce-Machine, he makes that machine as pliant, fluid, and unpredictable as Joyce's language. He seems to want a machine as soft as flesh or brain, acknowledging the role of language in its more unpredictable manifestations (275ff). Patricia Churchland, another philosopher of the machine mind, has devoted her career to the reduction of mental life to neural computation. She avoids Dennett's interesting complications by reducing language itself to a computational model, thereby assuring that the computer model will not come too strongly into conflict with language. But the problem with the machine model has everything to do with language. As structuralist analyses of language have made clear, the sustaining center of a structure – and language has a structure – is outside the structure: consequently, the speaking being cannot know that part of itself which is not within language.

If the brain were really a computer, even one too complicated for humans to decode within the lifespan of the species, it would remain in principle knowable, and we, like James's Maisie, would gradually learn more and more on the way to knowing all. What Dennett and Churchland, like many positivist scholars, cannot accept is that the real brain might have something about it that

16

ultimately resists symbolization and capture, which would mean that it would remain unknown. Their mistake is that they reverse the metaphor (the computer is a brain) to produce a fantasy (the brain is a computer). While a metaphor retains the mark of its construction as a limited fiction, the fantasy substitutes itself for reality. Slavoj Žižek links this mistake to a definition of the Lacanian Real: "the Real designates the very remainder which resists this reversal" (1993: 42), or alternatively, the Real is "a surplus, a hard kernel, which resists any process of modeling, simulation, or meta-phoricization" (44). Take a brain apart, model it, simulate it, and no consciousness emerges. So soft, so mutable are both brain and mind that neither is ever sufficiently stable to be fully known in either form or function. Unlike any machine, the brain's neurons fire on their own internal impulses in a chaos that only a theory of complexity might describe, exceeding any reduction to computational cause and effect.[8] The Real of consciousness would be that part of mind and brain that, because the brain is *not* actually a computer, cannot be fully, finally represented: it remains sublime. Our problem is how to explore this unrepresented excess.

The philosophers' arguments, strangely, include no discussion of either desire or pleasure, as if these things were unnecessary to the event we call consciousness. For Dennett's computer, there can ultimately be no question of desire, because he leaves no room for a lack, for a fundamental drive to repair the sense that something is missing. For although a computer could be turned toward a soluble problem, it could never solve the problem of human desire, which never ends with the acquisition of the object of desire. Once basic physical needs are satisfied – and what these needs are is not obvious – the sense of loss takes on a symbolic dimension. In Lacan's revision of the castration complex, he defines the phallus not as the answer to desire (it is not the power one wants, or the object that will satisfy) but as the signifier of lack; that is, not as the thing that is missing from our lives that leaves us unsatisfied, but as the sign that something is missing. The phallus always reminds you of your inadequacy. In reformulating the dynamic in this way, Lacan shifts the problem of desire from the lost *object* to the *fantasy* of loss: we long for the object of desire not because some primal object is missing, but because we cannot bear the emptiness defined by the limits of the Symbolic world. The phallus conceals the hole in the structure of representation, allowing us to deny what would otherwise be evident: complete satisfaction is impossible. The phallus is the fetish of the healthy psyche, which may explain why the healthiest of us is perverse at heart.

Of course, the hole in the Symbolic, though it may be nothing, is not empty: it is the place of the unrepresented Real. We seldom encounter this Nothing, however, thanks to the celerity of consciousness in presenting us with the phallus instead of nothing. Like Kant, we prefer the beautiful over the sublime, duty over "pathological" pleasure. Both beauty and duty arouse the subject to consciousness, that artful state of attention by which we claim a proprietary interest in knowing: *I* am thinking. But there is a paradox here that goes contrary to most conceptions we hold about consciousness: consciousness arises when something does not work. Lacan says that we speak of cause and effect only when the relation between the two events contains a mystery.[9] I don't, for example, say that my foot caused my shoe to move (unless I am a philosopher), though we might well question what caused my foot to move (muscle, reflex, will?). More generally, consciousness, I am arguing, is a response to such a gap in the symbolic structure, a response that turns us back on ourselves in a pulsing awareness that something obscure has fallen between what we are and what we know. Consciousness, that is, is the defense against that obscurity, a retreat to the formal boundaries of a self and to the security of meaning.

The play of the mind on the boundary between the Symbolic world and the Real produces what I am calling consciousness here. It arises where the Real impinges on representation. Gerald Edelman in his work on neural Darwinism argues that the brain develops neural pathways following a course of selection: those things that the brain does first and often are strengthened at the expense of little-used or merely possible pathways. The brain enjoys what it does well and will follow its enjoyment even when that enjoyment has no evident utility for the rational self, the subject of symbolic life. And this enjoyment, like Kristeva's *chora*, provides the base for "higher" mental functions long after we have lost direct contact with it.[10] Consciousness, then, contains the traces of neural events that persist beyond representation and to which we are ambivalently drawn. However, because those events precede representation, we can approach them only indirectly, through the mediation of symbolic life. And here we see something of the perverse nature of reason insofar as it is a form of symbolic representation: its primal (if not primary) function is to trigger the enjoyment that reason itself would avoid.

If the concept of enjoyment I am describing seems to retain a mechanical dimension, this machine works compulsively, oblivious and even opposed to the rational ends of the "operator," if that is what human consciousness is. If this machine is a computer, it is like HAL, the rogue computer in *2001: A Space Odyssey*, a machine its makers can no longer fully understand. HAL externalizes the sense that something not-I chugs along inside us that we do not control, even if we exploit it. Similarly, the "desiring machines" described by Deleuze and Guattari drive the organism without the need for conscious (or unconscious) motivation. And Brian Fawcett's "Reptile Machine" half-seriously explains that numerous human horrors are a product of an elemental paranoia that can be aroused in the "reptile brain" we each carry within our more sophisticated human brains (30–5). These "machines" suggest that something within human thought and passion remains beyond our knowledge, remains the uncanny obstacle to our attempts to master our fates. Although we live our conscious lives within the dimension of symbolic life, we are tied to a persistent, compelling past.

The question I intend this book to provoke is how one can prevent one's enjoyment, one's connection to a fixed past, from being appropriated by the projects of enlightenment, capital, nationalism, and related enterprises. To put the issue in other terms, I am arguing that we are not going to understand our pleasure, whether it comes in sublime or mundane forms, without acknowledging its relation to the perverse. The problem of agency with which I conclude this book asks how, given the deep involvement of reason with perverse enjoyment, one can act with any hope of breaking the cycles of violence that infect social relations. How might one refuse the cover stories that prevent us from accepting the fact of perversity in our motivations, how live in uneasy community with those around us?

2

THE SUBLIME COMMUNITY

At some point in many late-night conversations, my friends, most of whom are academics, have turned to the problem of community. The intimacy of such moments is no argument against the lament that we have no real community. We are, after all, most of us, Americans, which is to say that we are mobile, that we spent our youths (or the decade most of us devoted to earning degrees) someplace else, in situations where we did not socialize within the compulsive structures of couples and office gangs. In that youth, it has come to seem, some deeper, less structured, more authentic pattern informed social life. So we talk together and weave the mythic narrative of community, which is something more than good-old-days nostalgia. Rather, we express an ambivalence about community that is part of a fundamental American tension: fleeing compulsory society, we find some way to light out for the territories, where people unite freely. But once there, we again draw around us the strictures that had previously driven us from civilization. "Community," it turns out, refers both to a fantasy of a place we lost and hope to regain, and to the real, often agonizing condition of living in proximity with the separate bodies and minds of others. Having made the trip to the new world, Arthur Dimmesdale saw the surrounding forest compress the village of Salem into a dense mass that somehow was not the new Jerusalem he had hoped for. Although Hester Prynne's house on the margins of town drew to it those who testified to the failure of community, no one should imagine that the alternative community generated by the talk that took place in that house was more authentic than the one in which they lived their daily lives. Nor have my friends, building a momentary community around a shared conviction that something now is lacking, repaired by some inversion the very loss we pondered.

I recently witnessed a version of that loss in the *POV* documentary "Berkeley in the Sixties." As I watched, my reactions progressed from an amused nostalgia to an increasing anxiety and depression. How hopeful the protests against the House Un-American Activities Committee looked, as did the Free Speech Movement that emerged from it. The rapid slide down the slick marble steps of buildings in San Francisco and Berkeley as the police dragged protesters out looked more like an amusement park ride than police force. Those kids knew what was right because *they* were the Americans, schooled in the ideals of free speech and individual rights. In many ways the hallways full of determined, singing students looked like America at its brightest arising from the darkest period of the Cold War and McCarthyite terrorism. Having found their moment of American sublimity, those students displayed faces glowing with the pleasure of a selfless commitment. They saw themselves assuming the power of their country as a natural blessing. It all made sense. There was no Marxist critique of the social or economic order here but a renewed commitment to an American ideal without any impulse to theorize.

My anxiety emerged as activists turned toward the less tractable problems of racism and the war in Vietnam. One witness remembered that she was walking away from a celebration after the Free Speech Movement victory, proud of her actions, when Mario Savio said, "Now we have a war to stop." "What war?" she thought – 1965. The sublime moments were still possible, but increasingly they had less to do with that mythic American community of people and land than with the ecstasy of the riot, the militancy of Black America, and the commune of the Woodstock nation. The American themes of justice, equality, and individuality continued to inform the political debate, but as those ideals came up against the other America of wealth and power, the contradictions within the American idea – between spirit and money, for example, or justice and property – emerged and undermined the common pleasure that politics had previously provided. An uneasy coalition arose between activist idealism and countercultural euphoria, each providing a justification in politics or pleasure for the other but also concealing each other's limitations until they collapsed near the beginning of the next decade. There was no unitary political position that could address problems of war, race, and poverty. And the hangovers were getting worse with age.

It has, some argue, always been the impulse of Americans to see their political aspirations in terms of the sublime, beyond the pragmatic politics of the Old World. The genius, if I may, of Ronald Reagan – who as governor of California so angrily denounced the children of the '60s – was to call for the liberation of the child in corporate and consuming Americans when the '70s had left us feeling old and cranky. The economic wave encouraged business and buyers to submit to a rediscovered joy in the market and the mall, and to disregard the principle of restraint: that all pleasure is limited, as children learn so painfully in their first decade of life. But under the cover of a new American innocence, there emerged an unprecedented compulsion to serve the economic machinery in the name of private satisfactions. Jean Baudrillard, America's cool lover, had seen it coming as early as 1970 when he identified the pathological obligation to enjoy within the "fun-system" of consumption (1988: 48). The narrowly constrained pleasures of consumption, so contemptuous of the pleasures of countercultural bodily excesses, had the unhappy effect of producing wild wealth for those few who had mastered the material fork of the American fantasy and increasingly precarious economic lives for the rest. J. G. Ballard looked at America, also in 1970, and in a scandalous piece called "Why I Want to Fuck Ronald Reagan" identified the governor's bursting anal joy as his most seductive characteristic, one that was to be realized on a national level in the 1980s. The fun was blinding. Only when consumers "lost confidence" at the end of the decade, like aging libertines sadly looking over yet one more virgin, did Americans begin generally to realize that the fun was not properly ours, that our desires were not our own.

What I am considering here is the place of pleasure in the formation of communities, particularly in America. Consistently, the dependence of community on enjoyment goes unacknowledged, producing disturbing implications on both national and international levels. The pursuit of happiness has a calculable side to it – one can measure wealth, economic security, property – but its other face exceeds calculation, producing effects that can appear at any moment sublime or obscene: nationalism, for example, can produce both high art and genocide. The mingling of these two dimensions appears, for example, at the center of Don DeLillo's work. He has consistently explored the problem of pleasure that attends Western, Enlightenment thought. It is difficult for most Westerners, particularly those with 10 years and more of university training behind them, to imagine that the idea of the rational individual has not triumphed in the world, that other people are not fundamentally like us. The businessmen, CIA spooks, insurance agents, and other power brokers in *The Names* (1982) long for something beyond their rational selves; and yet they can no more imagine that a cult that kills people in accord with an alphabetic scheme represents the ways a majority of the world behaves than we believe David Koresh or Jim Jones represents the norm of American faith, though they may. In *The Names,* DeLillo represents what goes beyond the individual most spectacularly in the image of thousands of people circling the Kaaba in Mecca, a mass of people running for faith. He opens *Mao II* (1991) with a similar vision: thousands of couples in Yankee Stadium being married simultaneously by the Reverend Sun Myung Moon to partners they have just met. In both cases, the ecstasy people feel from submerging themselves in a human wave more than compensates for the loss of a distinct individuality. The shadow of that deep pleasure, where some infantile joy inhabits the idea of a community, haunts every attempt by DeLillo's characters to construct satisfying lives. No evidence of particular failures in Moonie marriages or alphabetic killings eliminates the desire DeLillo's Americans feel for some sublime transformation that would take them out of their separate lives and merge them with the infinite. DeLillo's project, which I take up, is to explore the consequences of being unable to distinguish between the fixable problems of social life – such as legal injustice or the economic exploitation of children – with the unfixable fact of human inadequacy, the condition psychoanalysis refers to as "castration." The failure to recognize this distinction, I argue, reflects a drive toward the harmonious community, toward a fantasy that has totalitarian unity as its conclusion.

Following the collapse of the Soviet Union and the subsequent reconfiguration of East–West power arrangements, it has become important on both domestic and international levels to figure out what will constitute a national pleasure – how are we going to understand community in a post–Cold War period when we can no longer simply unite against an evil power? And as we are regularly asked by our national leaders to rediscover America – always a provoking proposition – it might serve us well to think again about the community and the sublime, the fiction of the polis and the inviting abyss at its heart.

Community as we normally think about it, that close union of people bound by political and affective ties, has probably never existed as a working social reality. But as an idea, it has driven social theorists at least since *The Republic* to attempt to resolve the various impasses between desire and necessity, between fantasy and the public stage on which it must finally be played out. Emerson's vision of American community is as recognizable to armed militias in Montana as to the most liberal politician: he imagines a sublime meeting of authentic individuality with a transcendent political stream. In the image of the "transparent eyeball" from "Nature" and the eye as circle in "Circles," Emerson leaps like any god between the center and the circumference: he is everywhere and nowhere. The glory of Emerson's American is that he can be fully individual in the abandonment of any particular position, "foolish consistency," or subjective presence. Emerson's idea of community expresses the dissolution of individual boundaries so that even when the American of "The American Scholar" thinks, he is "Man Thinking," not a man, Being rather than a being in Heidegger's terms: "The world, – shadow of the soul, or *other me*, – lies wide around" (71). Emerson's essays read like the longings of a man and nation for ecstasy, for the thrill of becoming oneself by denying that the self has any limitation. The only suitable stage for his fantasy of transcendent enjoyment is the entire land, a staging that justifies every excess by being equivalent to nothing less than America itself, as Whitman later came to write of his own experience. This dream, which more appropriately expresses a person's relation to the smaller units of the family or tribe, has found a deep hold in American minds, encouraging a long series of patriots to forget they are not in actuality the USA.

The sort of contradiction implied in this conception of community is the subject of two of Steven Connor's recent books on contemporary theory and value, and as such the books serve as examples and analyses of the obsessions and repetitions that divide literary and cultural studies. What makes the British Connor useful for my analysis is that he thinks through these problems in terms of pleasure. He locates the theoretical divide along the difference between satisfaction (the end of a Freudian death drive) and ecstasy (the *jouissance* of the sublime), a difference that comes to mark the line between totalitarianism and anarchy. Connor articulates this opposition in *Theory and Cultural Value:*

> The experience of pleasure in art and culture may be a useful place to start, not because art and culture offer access to any kind of pure or disinterested pleasure, but precisely because of the uncertain and impure nature of pleasure in these areas, poised between the interested and disinterested, between use-value and exchange-value, between homeostatic ego-gratification and the indefiniteness of sublime pleasure. (54)

In laying out the nature of this "impure" pleasure, Connor articulates a rationale for using art to examine cultural issues. Art both embodies and represents a field of oppositions that Connor circles as he returns to the ripe topic of ethics: so much theory, but what do you do?

In his exploration of ethical positions, Connor does not let stand any plea for a paradise of resolutions, no Jürgen Habermas or Fredric Jameson opening a door to utopia, more or less. But he does repeatedly suggest that we might live ethically in the center of a vortex. While remaining skeptical of the university as an institution, for example, one could still retain a "principled attachment" to it as a center that holds crisis open for examination (130). Feminists might dialectically inhabit both a French field of difference and poetics (Luce Irigaray, Hélène Cixous) as well as a more political field of universals directed toward developing a "dynamic interplay" of values (186–7) and thereby remain ethically engaged. Theory, that is, should not determine values or evacuate them but chart the passage of values from one field of thought or action to another (257). Connor's compromise is not simply an appeal to American pragmatism, as much as he admires the school of thought that runs from John Dewey and William James to Richard Rorty. Rather, Connor seeks a determined suspension between idealism and daily life. But the suspension he produces inevitably sways toward the pole of ethical action, and Connor repeatedly abandons theory, leaving it to flounder in a pluralistic sea in which all ideas represent possible truths, and all are equally open to being dismissed. Like too many critics (not all) working in historicist and cultural studies, he displays an ultimate distrust of theory, which in its more austere late-twentieth-century forms tends to find all conclusions inadequate and refuses to grant any line of action a solid justification or any actor a clear conscience. What contemporary theory tells us is that every ethical position drags its dark Other along with it, its connection to a forgotten past. We must act, but we shouldn't imagine that any decision attains the purity of a Kantian imperative, untainted by "pathological" enjoyment. Like Connor, I seek a suspension, but one that practices a discipline of limitation. Literary interpretation, with its irresolvable conflicts, provides one way of approaching that practice.

Before turning to literary manifestation of such disturbing connections in the following chapters, I want to explore the territory as it is mapped by Jean-Luc Nancy and Jean-François Lyotard, two writers who follow the trail that runs between the abject and the sublime in human relations.

Essays that Nancy wrote in the mid-1980s emerge from the dilemma faced by the Left (that part of politics concerned "at least" with "what is at stake in community as opposed to the right's concern with order and administration" xxxvi) during the collapse of communism. The topical essays – on democracy, communism, freedom, religion, love – are couched in the difficult, deconstructive gestures of deferral typical of Martin Heidegger or Jacques Derrida. Despite a lack of historical detail, however, Nancy's claims about the future of communism as a social form go to the heart of dilemmas faced by Western culture. At the same time the Soviet Union disappears, communism ironically reemerges in the West in new forms, emblematic of "the desire to discover or rediscover a place of community at once beyond social divisions and beyond subordination to technopolitical dominion" (1). As Marx and Engels note in the opening of *The Communist Manifesto,* communism is the "spectre" of the capitalist West. But this ghostly double does not represent merely an economic counterforce. The very culture of the West evokes a dangerous longing for a union of the people, for a unified, archaic community. The most threatening social forms this fantasy takes, Nancy argues, are those of communities that "operate," that are deliberately "worked" out: religion in its more enthusiastic forms, nationalism, and other political movements that tend toward the production of a unified, communal spirit, all tending toward totalitarian impulses.[1]

What Nancy values instead is the "inoperative," "unworking," *désoeuvrée* in community, "that which, before or beyond the work, withdraws from the work, and which, no longer having to do either with production or with completion, encounters interruption, fragmentation, suspension" (31). That is, the community Nancy imagines is one that emerges from what resists the communal, the gathering of all people into an essential spirit. Nancy's community, by contrast with the communal, would be what "exposes" you to the fact of your singular, mortal self in the presence of others. Inoperative community would deter any Emersonian soul from thinking he had become one with all his land.

Nancy presses on the contradiction in democratic societies that Americans have learned to live with, although mostly by forgetting it exists: we dwell with, but separate from and antagonistic toward, others. Hannah Arendt, writing about America's revolution, notes a similar forgetting when she looks at the slip in Jefferson's language from a social and political bond based on "mutual promise" to one of "consent" (176). The difference is that consent implies the giving up of individual desires to an authoritative leader, whereas promise implies the agreement of people divided by their individuality to join together in spite of, and recognizing, their separation. The *promise,* Arendt argues, was the great American invention, *consent* the slide back to a European model, and what we lost in the shift of terms was the open willingness to live with difference. This loss has had discouraging consequences in recent years.

The Cold War period demanded that the capitalist democracies measure themselves against the claims of the Soviet Union. John Kennedy, debating Richard Nixon, for example, could advocate that America pursue social programs that resemble communism's ideals (economic opportunity and protection against the suffering accompanying poverty) only because the question of capitalism's superiority remained open: widespread poverty made us look bad.[2] But the post–Cold War period has brought us "the consensus of a single program that we call 'democracy' " (Nancy, xxxviii). Consensus has replaced the difficult, conflictual process of communication, just as communion (the union of spirit) has replaced community. Consequently, two great yet contradictory fantasies inhabit the national consciousness, producing heat without enlightenment. Americans tend to assume that we are all individuals, even though the only full individual is, literally, the dead individual (13), someone at last no longer touched by others. At the same time, the fantasy of a lost community lets us imagine a return to an earlier relation to others that was profoundly satisfying and unconflicted, to a "lost age in which community was woven of tight, harmonious, and infrangible bonds" (9). The problem with such communities, however, is that they suppress all freedom, community, and life, as contemporary examples almost anywhere in the world will demonstrate.

Real community, by contrast, involves "sharing" (*partage*), the fact of coming together that distributes, spaces, and places people so that it is not one's individuality that emerges, but a sense of individual "finitude":

> Sharing comes down to this: what community reveals to me, in presenting to me my birth and my death, is my existence outside myself. . . . A singular being *appears,* as finitude itself: at the end (or at the beginning), with the contact of the skin (or the heart) of another singular being, at the confines of the *same* singularity that is, as such, always *other,* always shared, always exposed. (26–8)

The skin, the face, the heart are for Nancy the simple physical facts that always limit our ability to merge with others, and no fantasy of communion – not even Nancy's own survival with a transplanted heart – will get past this difference. But these limits are also what open us to communication, to an awareness of our "exposure" before the world, and, crucially, to ecstasy, "what happens *to* the singular being" (7).

Hard work, of course, to face exposure, but this is the way to thought, to the divine, to love, to "the impossible." It is not wholeness but limits that Nancy seeks. Two passages on love:

> Love re-presents *I* to itself broken .... he, this subject, was touched, broken into, in his subjectivity, and he *is* from then on, for the time of love, opened by this slice, broken or fractured, even if only slightly.... From then on, *I* is *constituted broken.* (96)

> But it is the break itself that makes the heart.... The beating of the heart – rhythm of the partition of being, syncope of the sharing of singularity – cuts across presence, life, consciousness. That is why thinking – which is nothing other than the *weighing* or testing of the limits, the ends, of presence, of life, of consciousness – thinking itself is love. (99)

Nancy is attempting here to link the social situation of "being in common," of community and thought, to *jouissance.* Joy "is to be cut across," which requires an opening to others in "abandonment," in "destitution," without the protection of spiritualism and forgetting.

I want to distinguish Nancy's description of community as that which separates and places us from Michel Foucault's description of community under panoptic surveillance. Foucault's followers (unlike Foucault) often see this state of affairs as having oppressive implications. The Foucauldian subject is not congenitally singular but is created as singular by and for power, created as a subject of knowledge. And because anything that might exist before or outside of power and discourse remains by definition unknowable, there seems to be no alternative to what power has created, no escape, no freedom. A number of theorists – strikingly, for example, Judith Butler in *Gender Trouble* – have proposed strategies for evading power. Butler repeatedly attempts to demonstrate that a sexual body does not exist prior to discourse, but the weight of this repetition suggests a fury at the thought that some piece of nature, as Freud puts it, might be behind our discontent. Insistently, she points to the discursive origin of gender's malaise, disavowing organic imperatives and their representation in drives – as if it could not be that drives themselves make us unhappy.

"The epistemology of drive theory is junk," a non-Foucauldian opponent of that nature huffed at me and then spun away when I asked about drives. If our grief is only a consequence of discourse, just bad epistemology, then we might make it all right some day. By avoiding junk epistemologies (those which suggest that some significant things cannot be known, it seems), one need not fear being duped or not knowing. Butler's famous nonsolution is drag, the multiplication of gender positions that enables the individual to exploit the constructions of power, using them to subvert and evade power, using them, in fact, for pleasure. The strategy of drag suggests that the way out of the constraints of gender, the marketplace, and technology is to seize the position imposed by social power and exploit it, multiplying marketplaces and commodities, increasing the flow of information, accepting not a single gender but many until power cannot trace your movements. However, I cannot get my mind off the film *Paris Is Burning* and the image of a boy named Venus, dreaming of the day when he could replace drag with a sex-change operation, the rhetorical with the real, and thereby marry and settle down in the suburbs. Venus had no interest in subversion: he used drag to enter into the most conventional forms of culture, not to evade their compulsions. He died before achieving his transformation, and meanwhile drag has become fashionable, just another avenue for commodification. In both subversive and conforming drag, I find a desperate optimism, a hope that happiness may yet be possessed as a condition of daily life. But I also find the con artist inviting the gull to deny all limits to health, wealth, and beauty: buy this beauty system, and your life will be restored.

The con artist offers real pleasure, but pleasure is part of the problem. The pleasures of consumption constitute one of the primary seductions of capitalism, but consumption also produces a grinding labor that is the inverse of joy, filling your car with packages and your eyes with images that leave you hollow and addicted, ready for the world of self-help. When thinking about such pleasure in Western society, we should probably keep in mind the obsessive and destructive *jouissance* that Baudrillard finds in our shopping malls and highways, the compelling repetitions in American history that W. S. Burroughs describes in *Cities of the Red Night,* arising from the moment the first invaders hit Western shores. For them, *jouissance* is the engine of repetition and entrapment. Nancy's austere alternative also looks to *jouissance* as a form of resistance to the compulsions and delusions of culture, but his is a *jouissance* that faces the fundamental incapacity of the human mind and body. For instance, when he discusses literature (which he opposes to myth, the lost story, the founding fiction), he argues that its function is to interrupt every myth, community, and thought of mastery. He does not look for a subject that is either whole (the dream of perfection) or constructed (the promise of drag) but "broken or fractured," and hence open. The ecstasy achieved by a rigorous thinker might enable him to avoid the seductions posed by fantasies of fulfillment, but it does not ultimately address the more perverse temptations and rewards of modern institutions. Beneath the obvious satisfactions of capital, government, science, and even gender lie ancient enjoyments that remain vital, but mostly unconscious.

What Lyotard adds to this discussion is a description of the dynamics of these unconscious enjoyments. His claims in *The Postmodern Condition* (1984) about the ubiquity of discursive forces seem forgotten in his later work, *The Inhuman* (1991), where he explores a tension between two different ideas of what constitutes the human in humanity or, rather, what constitutes the inhuman limits of humanity. Lyotard situates the human between two "inhuman" temporal positions. One is the indeterminate movement of "progress," "development," or "complexification," a brute, evolutionary drive within the order of things toward order that produces our cities, industry, communications systems, and institutions, no matter what the cost to any species, our own included. Our human desires, the passions that we identify as our humanity, work largely, though unconsciously, in service to this "inhuman" drive, allowing us to imagine that we are fulfilling purely personal needs as we promote a larger complexity. The other temporal position is the static persistence of the lost animal, the "familiar and unknown guest" (1991: 2) from our infant past that haunts our dreams, language, and art. This second and more obscure inhuman informs our humanity and comes back to us in what Freud describes as repetition, remembering, and working through. Anamnesis, as a process of narrative remembering by which one comes to know that past, works counter to the drive toward progress: "writing and reading which advance backwards in the direction of the unknown thing 'within' " (3).

Lyotard sees us as caught between these two forces but with the possibility of choosing to work in the mode of one or the other. He favors the work of anamnesis (for which reading and writing are exemplary forms of such work, but not the only ones), although the direction of the civilized world is otherwise. Complexification, like the unification within Nancy's "working" (that is, not inoperative) community, like the Foucauldian extension of power, tends toward the reduction of specific humans to the components of a larger task, to the "hardware" of civilization. Lyotard would resist complexification, but not through a direct analysis of its forces in the hope of producing a counterpractice. Most of such resistant thought is itself an aspect of the drive toward complexity, and hence complicit with its end. Lyotard's counterintuitive approach conceives of a thinking without individual mastery. Although we think because we have bodies – the body is within thinking as "writing is in language" (17) – the body remains surprisingly impersonal. Other writers have attempted to theorize this body. When Jane Gallop offered us all a photograph of the birth of her son, she announced a new personal criticism that also denied the independence of the cogito from the bodily experience. In some of the critical writing that followed, however, personal experiences that were presented as the origin of thought effectively screened the real consequences of having a body: its weakness, inadequacy, and lack of control. What Gallop's picture reveals is just how much the simple fact of having a body produces the traumatic condition that originates thought. The bodily Real opens a troubling gap in the symbolic world. Lyotard's writing suggests that the most productive thinking recovers the traumatic body of childhood that informs powerful experience, that makes such experience more than a personal event. It is just this idea of the body that Nancy is speaking of – broken, open, exposed – which makes his ideal of "being in common" possible.

This approach implies, I think, that despite Butler's contention, gender is not the trouble but an answer (flawed as it may be) to the real trouble of having a body. Psychoanalysis invites us to consider what is at stake in this body: bodies are incomplete, born premature, divided by sex, mortal. These incomplete bodies are incapable of permanent satisfaction, and so we suffer. As Jacques Lacan, always the joker, puts it, there is no sexual relation: the desired, fantasized sexual union is always riven by internal divisions. Something unavailable to thought – Lyotard, like Lacan, calls it the Real – forever blocks the way to satisfaction. All consolations for the flaw this Real exposes in symbolic forms, from gender to philosophy, are doomed to fail and thus may sometimes seem more trouble than they are worth. But that does not keep us from continuing to try to find happiness through them. The irony here is that these flawed institutions – family, government, education, gender, and so on – continue to provide ancient, perverse enjoyments regardless of their inability to make us happy or their tending to make us miserable. And here is the heart of the problem.

The consequence of this perverse enjoyment for the modern world is a fatal repetition. America's enlightened armies of liberation continue to stumble into colonialism; gender refuses to be freed from romance; nations divorced from Soviet compulsion seek out atavistic identities defined by indignities suffered in previous millennia. For literary modernity, too, every *now* is burdened with the excess of an unspoken past and a future that provokes a "perpetual rewriting" (28) in which every event is subject to a return. For literature and history, the question is how that return occurs. It can be as the obsessive return of a crime of unconscious desire, endlessly repeated as though it were fresh each time. From Charles Brockden Brown through Poe, from Faulkner through Richard Powers, writers tell an American story of the endless surprise of the innocent man gouging out one more cat's eye, killing one more wife, loving one more sister, destroying one more child, once more, with feeling. These writers represent an unconscious impulse toward perverse enjoyment that links, for example, *The New Criterion*'s anxious con-

33

tempt for DeLillo's un-American novels and their relentless gaze at our national pastimes, to America's national hatred of the ethnic other, those merry laughing folk who in their poverty rob true Americans of their unnamable enjoyment. On the other hand, the return can come as the desire, like Oedipus', to control the past by discovering and acknowledging the crime, by closing in on it, which always leads one to repeat the form of the crime (29): this is the pathos of liberal pluralism, which allows us to recognize former crimes while participating in the pleasure of their commission (the shameful destruction of the native American people, as thrillingly represented, for instance, in *Dances with Wolves*), as the Wolf Man makes use of his Magic Word in analysis for continued enjoyment. In both forms of repetition, there remains the conscious hope that some original fault might be set straight or be so reformed that it ceases to antagonize us, while the labor of reform itself continues to provide us with an uncanny enjoyment.

Can there be a way out of this trap? Nancy's deconstructive suspension has so much renunciation of desire about it that one might detect the odor of the Kantian perverse in his method: true joy comes from the pain of duty, but only when it brings no overt pleasure. Lyotard, however, suggests that we pay attention not to the lost body of pleasure but to the "matter," the "body" that does speak: "The body is a confused speaker" (38), and because the body speaks unclearly, the orderly world ignores and thereby loses "the enigmatic confusion of the past, the confusion of the badly built city, of childhood . . . the disorder of the past which takes place before having been wanted and conceived" (38). The reasoning world has no interest in and derives no benefit from knowing such a past. The "inhuman" of complexification manifests itself unconsciously in the calculations of Enlightenment thought, capitalism, technology, and institutional life. Consequently, Lyotard claims, what we experience as desire is "no doubt no other than this process itself, working upon the nervous centres of the human brain and experienced directly by the human body" (71). Any thinking that follows the path of desire (in this case, desire for a stable understanding) is duped.

Fortunately, the other "inhuman," that of the confused body, is not silent. It exists, for one, in language where words are the body

34

of thought. Lyotard puts it this way: "Words 'say,' sound, touch, always 'before' thought. And they always 'say' something other than what thought signifies, and what it wants to signify by putting them into form. Words want nothing. . . . They are always older than thought" (142). Words are like that old, animal child-body that one can never be rid of: "Always forgotten, it is unforgettable" (143). Writing, then, points toward one kind of thought, *jouissance,* and the resistance to the inhuman process of capital and complexification. Lyotard makes no claim that this resistance will in itself ever liberate anyone, but here he does suggest an addition to the "empowering" strategies that give hope to many committed to social change. Where the fantasy of total empowerment is a delusion foisted on a credulous multitude of the resentful, Lyotard would have us listen to the words, to understand what forgotten body is being stirred, and for whom it is being roused. And for America, still so committed to the fresh start, there might be some virtue in recognizing that visions of a sublime future take their form from an abject past.

Modern communities will, of course, continue to be plagued by too much mindless suffering, boredom, and violence. And always there are the temptations offered by those who would relieve us of the suspense of our lives through the promised ecstasies of religion, consumption, nationalism, or family. But the political solutions suggested by optimistic versions of Foucault, by an open, pragmatic pluralism, or by the wish for a social unity that characterizes much political discussion often lead nowhere because they participate in a pattern of thought that denies what cannot be clearly, positively articulated. Much historical and cultural criticism, that is, has increasingly rejected theory and interpretation, abandoning "impractical" textuality in favor of undeniable fact. Even some psychoanalytic criticism, for example, in its turn toward self-psychology and object relations, disavows the bodily Real and its inarticulate forces in the hope of finding an accidental, hence correctable, cause of human or social unhappiness: your mother, just for example, was not sufficiently empathetic to you. As if they can no longer stand the limited and unheroic role of interpreting the world, critics of literature, culture, history, and mind have begun to act out an understandable desire to fix things. But too often they confuse, I believe, the unhappiness that comes from social and economic injustice, which may respond to action, with the unhappiness that arises in the meeting of the human with the inhuman in us. This is not a condition to fix but one to understand and turn to useful thought and work.

The problem one faces in any attempt to alter sublime phenomena is that their unapproachable dimension, the grandeur of great happenings, transcends our capacity for representation. Additionally, the inertial power of American institutions exalts those who find themselves riding that great power. The thrill felt by buyers and sellers striving on the floor of the stock exchange looks to many comparable with that which drives the masses DeLillo describes, those who marry by the ballparkful and pray in swirling multitudes. Neither intellectual analysis nor performative acts of resistance to dominant institutional power are going to provide a counterpleasure to substitute for the ecstasy these people experience – not unless such acts touch sources of the perverse equal to those aroused by the sublime.

If we will be happy, then, it will not be in the community of consumption or in a Foucauldian resistance to such communities. Lyotard suggests that in an attention to language there may be some relief for the sad animal of humanity, and perhaps here there is the suggestion of another literary and critical practice that is not fated to repetition:

> We wake up and we are not happy. No question of remaking a real new house. But no question either of stifling the old childhood which murmurs at our waking. Thinking awakens in the middle of it, from the middle of very old words, loaded with a thousand domesticities. Our servants, our masters. To think, which is to write, means to awaken in them a childhood which these old folk have not yet had. (197)

The pleasures Lyotard describes here are, significantly, domestic – the foundation, not the end, of social practice. As humans, our first extra-uterine contact with the body of another is accompanied by language, as if language is the first compensation for separation. If we are to understand our relations to others, the attractive force we call community, we should pay attention to the capacity our symbolic world has to stir these old children. Lyotard names this

36

attention "writing," though I will generalize it to include all activities that enable this attentive work, from digging up the stones of past civilizations to remembering one's dreams.

As with all children, the question is not whether they will obey, but whom? What kind of community will enlist the polymorphous body of pleasure if you do not embrace it as your own? Can one avoid the trap of communal totalitarianism and attain Nancy's arduous community of separate people, and still produce the enjoyment necessary to survival? It is worth remembering that ethical actions depend on the drives toward enjoyment that give them force, even as they tend to screen that dependence. Such drives, with their impulse toward repetition, need to be acknowledged, lest they covertly rule all action. When J. G. Ballard looks to the Manson family as an explanation for why children leave home, or when Don De-Lillo represents the passionate communities of cults, religions, nationalists, and agents (of all kinds), they are looking at the power of language to move a body beyond all reason, to evoke the sublime by an appeal to the perverse. The rest of this book will demonstrate how such an appeal has functioned in one strand of American literature.

3

RE-POE MAN
POE'S UN-AMERICAN SUBLIME

Ordinary fucking people. I hate them.
Repo Man

Americans tried to bury Poe, but the French dug him up. Like the plots of Poe's stories, the American coverup was too shallow to conceal the entire body of his work, and so the telltale part resurfaced, arousing both disgust and delight. Like the teeth of Berenice, torn from the prematurely buried body of the young woman, some hard kernel of pleasure remained all the more certainly available to later readers for Poe's having been disposed of so early. The French preserved him for us, so that when we weary of the story of American grandeur, of the country's special and sublime role in history, we can return to the closeted pleasures of the small, secret places of the past. When we see the lapses in the national story, when we suspect we have been diddled, we dig up Poe.

The problem with Poe for the American canon, at least in part, is that he implicitly denies the scale of the national enterprise with his short, compulsive tales. While the Emersonian subject aspires toward the transcendental, to a condition beyond the limited body of the individual person, Poe's obsessional subjects seldom look beyond the immediate – the object, person, or event that imagination has seized upon and filled with dread. The linked endeavors of the Enlightenment and Romanticism had worked to free desire from the tyranny of the personal. The free thinker could think with the detached clarity of a reason that depended on no earthly authority –

Dupin impersonates such a thinker. Similarly, the emotion aroused by a particular event for the Romantic depended on its connection to a greater spirit that informed maid and mountain. But Poe's work denies the central significance of such ideas, displaying thinking and emotion – in tales of reason, tales of horror – to be bound to the stupid Real. He shows the transcendental subject to be a version of the subject of enjoyment.

Fortunately for Poe's critical standing, the seemingly austere practice of poststructural criticism returned America to the text in a way that New Criticism never could. The text as urn or icon, for all its apparent materiality, remained for this American school an opening to the sublime, an access to unvoiced realms of the human experience, generally more wonderful for being otherwise unnamable. The poststructuralists, however, fixed on words, exposing their irreducible materiality, their dependence on readers to mean anything at all, much less something sublime. They "played" with the old masters' words. Clearly, they took too much pleasure in a task that brought no profit. They began enjoying Poe's words, as the narrator of "Berenice" enjoys teeth.

The story of "Berenice," briefly, is of a recluse who inhabits a library while his beautiful cousin, Berenice, lives in the sun. He suffers from "monomania" and takes an interest in her only when she begins to sicken, all of her body shriveling except her teeth. These teeth become the center of his monomania, the things without which, he believes, he cannot regain reason. Finally, she is buried, at which point he goes, not knowing what he does, to her tomb, where he pulls out the teeth of the still-living Berenice.

The specific perversion of the narrator, Egaeus, involves books. He speaks of its origin in the library, one evidently lacking American classics: "The recollections of my earliest years are connected with that chamber, and with its volumes – of which latter I will say no more. Here died my mother. Herein was I born" (225). All the "dissipations" of his youth, all his pleasures, are in the library. Significantly, his attachment to the room comes with the early loss of his mother and those primal pleasures associated with her. His "reveries" over books and words in the library, however, begin at some point to take on a different, more distressing character as "monomania": a "nervous *intensity of interest* with which, in my case,

39

the powers of meditation (not to speak technically) busied and buried themselves, in the contemplation of even the most ordinary objects of the universe" (227). His contemplations lead him, for example, "to repeat monotonously some common word, until the sound, by dint of frequent repetition, ceased to convey any idea whatever to the mind" (227). Like a deconstructive reader, he shifts his attention from signification to the material object, a practice that separates him from the realm of healthy readers (those reading to find the meaning) and healthy lovers (those looking for their true mate). As if he sees that those who follow their hearts are condemned to the delusions of desire, to the pathways of endless deferral, he refuses such a life and fixes his attention on one absorbing object. His passions, he says, "*had never been* of the heart [but] *always were* of the mind" (229). How many critics inspired by Derrida have been condemned for heartless readings?[1]

I had the opportunity to watch a group of undergraduates listening to this story being read aloud, and their attention wavered during Egaeus's (the narrator's) passionate discussion of his reading. But when his monomania became attached to Berenice's teeth, the listeners were suddenly galvanized. Rather than speaking of books' being opened, Egaeus speaks of Berenice's shrunken lips' parting to reveal "a smile of peculiar meaning [when] *the teeth* . . . disclosed themselves slowly to my view" (230). The texts of this library give way to the simple if "ghastly *spectrum* of the teeth." The weirdness of this mania invites an amused and fascinated, if disapproving, reaction. In place of the arcane ideas Egaeus had pursued, the teeth in their unspotted whiteness seem to represent a more intensely present meaning. Egaeus says that while "[Of] Mad'-selle Sallé it has been well said, '*que tous ses pas etaient des sentiments*,' [that all her steps were feelings] . . . of Berenice I more seriously believed *que tous ses dents etaient des idées*' " [that all her teeth were ideas] (231). The shift from the white page of his books to the white teeth of Berenice is in fact less a change in interest for Egaeus than a continuation of the specific perverse interest he had always shown: the pages were always simply the teeth, like those in his dear mother's reading mouth.

Egaeus's unconscious extraction of Berenice's teeth appears as a "fearful page in the record of my existence, written all over with dim, and hideous, and unintelligible recollections" (232). This page, like the teeth, is suggestive but obscure. The emotion aroused by it remains beyond any meaning, yet powerful. When Egaeus is aroused from his stupor, his eyes "dropped to the open pages of a book," to a poem that directs him to visit his beloved's tomb if he would find relief from sadness. He then notices his bloody clothes and that his hand is "indented with the impress of human nails." And on the table beside him is a box containing "thirty-two small, white and ivory-looking substances" (233). Too literal a reader, Egaeus has in fact gone to the tomb, wrestled with the prematurely buried Berenice, and brought the teeth back to the library, like an overdue book. In the process, his hand has been "impressed," and we read in those "indentations" the presence of *les dents*. The connection between page and the body emerges in this image of writing and teeth, and we see how books had served to reassure Egaeus that enjoyment would not be limited by his mother's death. But when he takes the teeth, he slips from the socially accepted fetish to the earlier, more abject one, denying death by capturing the smile of the dead woman.

Poe claims that the real interest of poetry is the suggestion of "supernal" beauty to be found there; but this story, at least, identifies the supernal not with the transcendent but with the repetition of a pleasure originally located in a now-lost maternal body. The story is not motivated by a desire for something unattainable, a represented thing pointed to by every sign. Neither were those young listeners interested in a mystery waiting to be resolved, in a hidden truth. They did not, that is, come to attention because the story had begun to move ahead – nothing really happens until the last page – but because it had begun to linger, to focus without the excuse of suspense on the moment of excitement and dread attached to an inconsequential insertion of a body part into the text. It is Egaeus's refusal to go beyond the body that holds a fascinated reader. The supernal, then, would be something like the Real, not a realm beyond language, but something in the present world that is left over, unrepresented by language. And unlike the Romantic who, in his desire, wishes that language with its inevitable limits would vanish so that the perfection imagined beyond language could be reached, the pervert seizes on the word, the part that in its physical presence disavows the loss of which the symbolic always reminds us.

Egaeus, in disavowing the love of Berenice, escapes this loss that kindles the passion of normal love; he chooses instead a passion outside of time and bodily decay, one with its present pleasures and all-too-evident horrors. The story he tells incorporates something of this disavowal. The readerly impulse to understand meets the obstacles of the narrative's failure to move forward, a stasis that compels a shift from understanding to collaboration, from critical or sympathetic desire to fascination. When Poe inserts teeth in the place of text, he invites an unhealthy interest, but one protected from the censoring faculty by the certainty that it is Egaeus, not we, who indulges monomanias, that it is merely text, not teeth, we are playing with. Within the normal narrative lies this textual indentation that flouts the law of meanings and endings, offering instead the pleasure of watching, lingering over what would otherwise offend us. This is what I am trying to describe as the perverse narrative.

We like our fictions to end with all accounts squared, as in marriage and death, though Poe leans toward the latter. Many of his tales end in imminent death – or even in posthumous narration as in "Ms. Found in a Bottle" and *The Narrative of Arthur Gordon Pym* – apparently demonstrating the claim made by Freud in *Beyond the Pleasure Principle* that all life tends toward a return to an earlier, inanimate state. Our lifelong struggles for knowledge, power, satisfaction, and certainty lead inevitably to the dust from which we arose. Or as John Irwin says of *The Narrative of Arthur Gordon Pym*, "we see the quest for fixed certainty . . . for what it is – a death wish" (1980: 235). But it is difficult to know what a death wish really means in practical terms. When Irwin returns to Poe in a later book, the quest has become a more formal matter, the staging of mysteries that allow for endless doublings and repetitions from story to story, from Poe to Borges and beyond. As he says of the problem of thinking, "there will always be one more step needed in order to make the act of thinking and the content of thought coincide" (1994: 12). Freud, it also appears, knew he was in trouble with the death drive throughout *Beyond the Pleasure Principle:* Why is the death drive so slow? Why is the arousal (called "unpleasure") produced by repetition sought so much more fiercely than satisfaction, the extinction of "unpleasure"? The pattern in Poe's stories seems to suggest that desire is divorced from truth, and "unpleasure" is its own reward: characters pursue paths with a perverse insistence that has little apparent motive. Pursuit and perversity: following and turning away, digging up what was buried. For Poe, the move toward death leaves nothing squared.

In the film *Repo Man,* the old pro – old con, rather – sits with his protégé watching people arguing in a parking lot and comments, "Ordinary fucking people. I hate them." He hates them because they are always trying to get out of tense situations. Not your repo man. He has an interest in tense situations that we would have to call perverse. Jean Clavreul, noting that "on the whole, erotic literature has been made up of writings by perverts," comments on the banality of ordinary people fucking: "from the point of view of eroticism, the 'normal individual' is presented, next to the pervert, as an inept yokel unable to raise his love above a routine" (216). The pleasure of perverts begins where ordinary peoples' imaginations stop dead. It is only when some repo man takes away the practical adult model we received in exchange for the dangerous pleasures of polymorphous youth that we get one more spin, one more peek into childhood's crypt.

In his exploration of the crypt, Jacques Derrida says some things that could help explain this unsettled nature of buried pleasures. "The inhabitant of a crypt is always a living dead, a dead entity we are perfectly willing to keep alive, but *as* dead" (xxi). The crypt, that is, does not finally rid us of something but preserves it where it will remain safe, neither dangerous nor endangered. In the particular case of Freud's "Wolf Man," which inspires Derrida's analysis, the encrypted thing is a word that preserves a dangerous pleasure resting in the Wolf Man's presymbolic past: "It is the very tombstone of the illicit, and marks the spot of an extreme pleasure [*jouissance*], a pleasure entirely *real* though walled up, buried alive in its own prohibition" (xxxiv, translator's brackets). The burial here does nothing to return the Wolf Man to some inertial quietude of death. On the contrary: "The very thing that provokes the worst suffering must be kept alive. The outpouring of the libido at the moment of

43

loss (whose intensity sometimes rises to the point of orgasm) is repressed, not in and of itself, as such, but in its ties with the dead" (xxxv). The crypt provides access to this intensity, "the corpse of an exquisite pleasure, disguised . . . as an exquisite pain," horrible but impossible to give up.

The crypt here is not the dark alterity of a structuralist Freudian unconscious, but a heterogeneous difference within the body over which the "Self [stands as] a cemetery guard" (xxxv). The Self, the representative of consciousness, makes sure that what is buried stays buried, yet available for repossession. Poe's narrators are such guardians, reasonable in the midst of their own excitement and fear, determinedly stupid about the treasures they protect. But as guards they are more con artist's shills than guides to lost time. They stand – and sometimes make us stand – as upholders of the law who nevertheless, in secret, watch what should not be seen. Reason and the law are the foundation of a civilized life, in relation to which Poe's perversions are unhealthy deviations, cautionary tales. But the fascination of the accomplice – the priest, the doctor, the reader – allows Poe to turn reason and law into the props for perverse pleasures. This inversion of priorities makes Poe's madmen the most insistent advocates of the law. They must, in fact, simulate a normal world in order to protect, hide, and produce the pleasures that this world ostensibly condemns. They are not the sort of friends whom the upholders of the law and canon can afford to keep.

Life in the Crypt

The narrator of "The Premature Burial" is one such cemetery guard who staidly invites us to contemplate encrypted things. He opens by noting that tales of horrible events hold a "legitimate" interest so long as they are based on real events: "it is the history which excites" (666). Only the vulgar would read of such events if they were mere fiction. The narrator permits an exercise in morbid curiosity to "those who think" (the refined), at once flattering and titillating readers. In the spirit of science, several pages of "true stories" follow on the topic of premature burials, "the most terrific of these extremes which has ever fallen the lot of mere mortality" (666). These stories, as interesting as they may be in themselves, merely introduce his case, his own premature burial.

The narrator's experience establishes his authority on the topic, something particularly important in light of his insistence on the *fact* of these stories. (In *The Narrative of Arthur Gordon Pym* the narrator makes a similar, though more extreme, claim, recounting experiences that are "the allotted portion of *the dead* . . . never to be conceived" (1153), a claim that is literally impossible to make.) "My own case differed in no important particular from those mentioned in medical books" (673), he says of his catalepsy, emphasizing the pathological ground of his fears of premature burial. As a consequence of his illness, he implies, his "fancy grew charnal," and he frequently dreams of death and prepares for it. Neither we nor he therefore is surprised when he awakens from his familiar catalepsy (no "ordinary sleep") to find himself in a grave. But he is mistaken. He is only in a berth in a boat. He was only sleeping soundly, better than usual, in fact. Does this lessen his authority to speak of the experience of premature burial? "The tortures endured, however, were indubitably quite equal, for the time, to those of actual sepulchre" (679).

Indubitably. Whether one is actually buried or not, the specific excitement he describes, and probably the excitement he would have experienced, is a fantasy derived from his reading. Like Egaeus, he has been aroused by his library: he reads "Buchan," *Night Thoughts,* and other morbid books, claiming he does so only to satisfy his legitimate curiosity. Legitimate or not, the narrator writes on his topic with as much authority as that of the sources he consults, which is very little. In one account of premature burial, people hasten to a funeral "on account of the rapid advance of what was supposed to be decomposition" (667) in a man actually alive. Such observers are as trustworthy as a man who fails to recognize Madeline Usher's blush as a sign of life. Horror, it seems, is aroused at least as easily by fiction as by horrific events, and therefore the effect is no guarantee that the cause was horrible.

The story's conclusion acknowledges one explicit confusion of cause and effect when the narrator says his catalepsy vanished with his apprehensions, which may have been "less the consequence than the cause" of his disease. In fact, the entire story undermines the distinction between cause and effect, a distinction that is one of the fundamental indicators of reality: we know things are in the realm of physical reality when our thoughts cannot affect them. And if there is no distinction between physical reality and thought, then the opening statement about the universal interest people show in horrific stories can make no claim about the "sanctifying" quality of truth: true or not, the stories are "all-absorbing." They are the crypts, the berths in which death is lived. This entire story, in fact, is about the "pleasurable pain" the narrator feels upon being absorbed by the tales, "devoured" by his fancies. The subject of Reason is indistinguishable from the perverse subject, one fixated upon a fantasy from his past and, to judge by his reading, his society's.

All the narrator's charnel fancies, his dreams of death, his "perpetual horror" and unstrung nerves are an extension of the pleasure of reading, a part of the reading itself. He does not read to reach a settled understanding any more than he strives toward his own actual death. To draw close to death in reading or action does not put an end to the "unpleasure" of aroused life but heightens anxiety, horror, and enjoyment. You want death; you don't want to be dead. The denials Poe's characters express about their fascination with death mimic on some level the tensions in Freud's thought in *Beyond the Pleasure Principle* as he tried to theorize a sex drive, Eros, to counter Thanatos. Perhaps the tension arises less from the two drives' being in conflict than from their being the same drive. The problem may be that life is as unthinkable as death: that is, just as the personal extinction that is death remains beyond the limit of knowledge except in its representations and effects, so "sex" (and the life it makes possible) is knowable only as a representation. For example, when F. R. Leavis identified the important quality of good literature, healthy literature, to be Life, he effectively placed it beyond understanding. "Life" was sublime, and Leavis's *Scrutiny,* as Terry Eagleton points out, "made a virtue out of not being able to define" it (42). Life itself evades us, but the wish for "death," for oblivion, always contains a reference to life's unspeakable force. And so the narrator of Poe's story claims in the conclusion that he overcame his compulsion (he stopped reading) and thereby put his demon to sleep, though the very existence of the "bugaboo tale" he writes suggests he is not done with horror stories. Moreover, his failure to recognize fully how absorbing terror is for him, his seeing the problem more simply as an overexposure to exciting stories (as cause rather than effect), leaves him open to a revival of his demon. The story seems, in fact, intended to reproduce the narrator's own state in his readers by offering the account of his experience.

The narrator's failure here to overcome his compulsion suggests a resistance to some knowledge for which the debilitating response of "horror" is a kind of screen. The story's conclusion sets this horror in opposition to health: an indulgence in fantasy can be cured by a return to the real world – exercise, travel, nature. Horror refers to an effect produced by something left undefined in the bright vision of work and reason, something that opposes the clear distinctions of life and death, cause and effect, reality and imagination. The turn toward horror denies the obligations of health, logic, and clarity, although it depends on them to produce its effects, its intense thrill.

But the narrator claims that horror is caused by something real: "The grim legion of sepulchral terrors cannot be regarded as altogether fanciful" (679). This implies that there is a realm not necessarily in opposition to waking life, but in competition with it, another kind of reality with its own appeal, distinct from anything offered (or refused) by health. The general interest aroused by stories of terrible events may, in fact, lead to a morbidity destructive to ordinary life, to a preoccupation with "charnal" (i.e., bodily) matters to the exclusion of the business of culture.

The opening of Michel Foucault's *Discipline and Punish* with its account of torture and the law's hold on the body points, as Nietzsche had earlier, to a communal enjoyment that had to be renounced for modern culture to arise.[2] The popular delight in blood stood in the way of the mass organization required by the emerging industrial world. The American Revolution, meanwhile, announced that a rationally organized community of men had formed who set their life, liberty, and happiness against the Old World. The American scholar, eager to throw off the dark, secretive, and bloody tradition of European power, would avoid the feelings of dread, revulsion, fear, and nausea that went with that tormented body and would choose health. While he mimicked the discourse of

47

reason, Poe lingered over that body, though he was unable to make the step W. S. Burroughs would and conceive of a community bound together by the perverse enjoyments of the body.

Family Life

The narrator's evident failure to choose health, despite insistent claims of sanity, presents the interpretive problem in several stories. "Why *will* you say that I am mad?" the narrator of "The Tell-Tale Heart" asks, when he can demonstrate the care and method with which he kills, dismembers, and hides the old man. Like "The Black Cat" and "The Imp of the Perverse," this story plays on the connection between an observer or reader who knows the difference between madness and sanity and a pervert driven toward a dangerous excitement. As they lay out the sequence of events that led them to their present situations, the narrators claim that "mere household events" are all a reader need be familiar with – the rough day, the wife/father/pet that gets on your nerves – to understand why, despite being good-natured, loving men, they commit a few murders. The telling aspect of their stories, however, is the excitement they betray as they confess.

The narrator of "The Tell-Tale Heart" has an "acuteness of the senses," something "you mistake for madness" (557). Night after night he goes to the door of the old man and looks in at the closed eye, feeling the pleasure of his "own powers – of my sagacity," the "triumph" of his planning. But he couldn't do the "work" (killing) until the eye is open and the old man terrified. As he waits to murder the man, he hears a groan:

> the low stifled sound that arises from the bottom of the soul when overcharged with awe. I know the sound well. Many a night, just at midnight, when all the world slept, it has welled up from my own bosom, deepening, with its dreadful echo, the terrors that distracted me. I say I knew it well. I knew what the old man felt, and pitied him, although I chuckled at heart. (556)

For what he calls a long while, he lets this feeling build in him in a mimetic tension until he leaps and kills. What strikes me here is not

48

the release of repressed violence but the careful and deliberate arousal of a sensation he equates with awe, an overwhelming state in which joy and terror are indistinguishable. The eye – the representation of the Father's gaze, the law, the phallus (to follow out Lacan's logic) – fails here to function as the limiting principle. The narrator projects his anxiety on this eye, investing it with extraordinary powers, just as any child will believe the parental organ of sight to be capable of penetrating vision. But rather than submitting to this limiting power, he denies it.

Following the murder, he is unwilling to lose this excitement, and in his "wise precaution" he buries the man in his own floor, beneath his chair, as if, like Usher, he could not bear to have the cause of his horror too far away. When the police enter to investigate, he begins to hear a sound like a muffled "watch," and as they talk he paces "as if excited to fury by the observations of the man" (559). The old man's eye is hidden, but the situation the narrator has arranged leads to a *watch* and *observations,* puns that return him to the excitement of the earlier gaze of the evil eye. He exercises the extreme acuity of his senses in detecting a heart that beats exactly like his own, and he ultimately reveals the body to the police, not because he feels guilty, but because they see: "they *knew!* – they were making a mockery of my horror! . . . Anything was more tolerable than this derision" (559). To the observing police, he looks like someone wracked by guilt, confessing because the eye of the law aroused his conscience. And to the observant reader, a similar conclusion would be likely. And so three times – in the old man's doorway, in the presence of the police, and in telling his tale – the narrator arranges observers, others who know and drive him to action. But the very ease with which we all know, all see the repressed workings of conscience, leads us to ignore this arranging, the setup in which observers participate in the narrator's excitement.

Clavreul notes the role the priest plays in voyeurism when hearing the pervert's confession: "Through a ritual gesture surely denuded of sense for the penitent, there is the assurance that someone who has an affirmative relation to the Law looked at his voyeurism with a blind look because he was secretly fascinated and thus an accomplice" (229). The reasonableness of police and readers, if not of the narrator himself, preserves and conceals the source of pleasure, allowing it to be reproduced at will. What the "normal" partner in the "perverse couple" doesn't understand is that his willingness to watch, to listen, to save the pervert from his unnatural pleasure and return him to health continuously reconstitutes the disavowal that marks the pervert's relation to pleasure and the law. Consequently, the pervert must keep his accomplice enthralled.

The narrator of "The Black Cat" not only claims he is sane but also asks his reader ("some intellect more calm, more logical") to find in these "mere household events" "nothing more than an ordinary succession of very natural causes and effects" (597). But the problem of cause is at the heart of the story: what has caused this new desire, one that leads a man known for his tender heart, docility, and humanity to become a killer? "I knew myself no longer," he says as he cuts his cat's eye out. He had married in one sense his double, a woman who "possessed, in a high degree, that humanity of feeling which had once been my distinguishing trait" (602). She is his mirror. But when she looks at him, her eye, like that of the old man in "The Tell-Tale Heart," becomes the gaze, that overwhelming presence of what Lacan calls the "subject supposed to know" (1978: 224 ff.). The gaze, Lacan makes clear, is not real – no father's eye can really see into the hidden truth of the child's desire – but is something that arises from the Real, from an unrepresentable but insistently disturbing source, which makes it as dreadful as it is exciting.

In describing the origin and development of his great humanity, the narrator never speaks of virtue and seems to feel little but contempt for "mere *Man*." He cared for animals, feeding and caressing them, and from them, he says, "I derived . . . one of my principle sources of pleasure." It is fine, of course, to be kind to animals, and the pleasure of the "self-sacrificing love of a brute" has a simplicity that human love seldom attains. But when he picks up his cat Pluto to cut out an eye, his act "thrilled every fiber of my frame": "I blush, I burn, I shudder, while I pen the damnable atrocity" (599). He feels shame, remorse, horror at his deed, I suppose. But his body, even when merely recounting the event, reacts as if wracked with the most intense pleasure. The two responses are evidently one.

What is remarkable is the lack of conflict between these two manifestations of a drive that leads him to care for and kill cats.

There is no guilt, but "a half-sentiment that seemed, but was not, remorse" (601). Horror predominates over guilt, and his actions seem directed toward reproducing the horror. When the hated cat is dead, he looks for its double, and so the sense of horror remains fresh, arousing him again to the frenzy that leads to murder. There is no better evidence for this drive toward repetition than the completely improbable circumstance of having unknowingly walled up the cat with his wife's body. Too clearly, he has found a way to keep the cat, alive but entombed. Like Montresor in "The Cask of Amontillado," he places the one who has done him a "thousand injuries" (848) where he is least forgettable.

When the narrator of "The Black Cat" speaks of "perverseness," he speaks of it both as a "primitive impulse," a "primary faculty" that defines "man" and as a secret rationality: "Who has not, a hundred times, found himself committing a vile or silly action, for no other reason than because he knows he should *not?*" (599). In "The Imp of the Perverse" the narrator also speaks of a primitive impulse – "elementary," but again secretly reasonable: "In theory, no reason can be more unreasonable; but, in fact, there is none more strong" (827). We are prevented, he says, from noticing this perverse rationality because of "the pure arrogance of the reason" (826). The narrator of "The Black Cat," for example, claims to be "above the weakness of seeking to establish a sequence of cause and effect" (600) (although he is "logical" enough to imagine that the dead cat ended up in the burning house because someone had thrown it through the window, "with the view of arousing me from sleep"). Our denial of rational motive, the narrators suggest, merely conceals a motive from consciousness, one whose reason would be too offensive to recognize.

"The Imp of the Perverse" describes a man standing on "the brink of a precipice" drawn by the thought of what it would feel like to fall: it "chills the very marrow of our bones with fierceness of the delight of its horror" (829). At the opening of "A Descent into the Maelstrom," the "old man" leads the narrator to the edge of a cliff, saying he "can scarcely look over this little cliff without getting giddy" (432) and then hangs precariously over the edge, "exciting" the narrator – and evidently himself. The old man had, in fact, plunged over the edge in his "descent," and the experience engraved something so deeply in him that he lives, it seems, to repossess it, in both action and story.

The desire of the perverse is not, here, "primary," but neither is the law a prior restraint forbidding the act. This "unfathomable longing of the soul *to vex itself*" (599) seems, on the contrary, to develop a concealing cloak of "should not" around the emerging desire. The stories indicate that some event established a path of bliss, of a horror so arousing that the teller of the story needs to return to that event to recover the feeling. But a plunge into a maelstrom is an event not likely to be often repeated. For most of us, the "reality principle" provides a mechanism for avoiding disaster while deferring the attainment of some desired object. The elaboration of this principle essentially structures oedipal organization with all the evasions and displacements that allow the desirous child to become a useful adult, though one fated to perpetual dissatisfaction. The pattern of the stories read here suggests a different, or at least an additional, mechanism. Oedipal repression depends upon the existence, real or imaginary, of the law – of nature, society, or the "soul" – forbidding the subject's desire. But in these stories the law is denied, negation negated: the soul vexes itself; the narrator of "Imp" runs through the street shouting out his guilt, just as the narrators of "The Black Cat" and "The Tell-Tale Heart" reveal their secrets to the police. Conscience, police, and nature all continue to punish these transgressors with little regard for motives, and with no appreciation of the possibility that they may be playing into other designs.

The narrator of "Imp" confesses his story with "passionate hurry, as if in dread of interruption" (831), and then he swoons. In "The Black Cat" he swoons and staggers in an "extremity of terror and of awe" (606) and confesses. The narrator of "The Tell-Tale Heart" foams and raves until the confession bursts from him. And even the successful narrator of "The Cask of Amontillado" needs the reader to enjoy with him that jingling of Fortunato's cap from behind the wall. Police and readers receive a confession but have no *reason* to see that in their witnessing they enable the speaker to feel a thrill that repeats something of the original experience. The structure of perversion in Poe suggests that the law as it has developed not only represses the desire for an object with its "should not" but also preserves an experience of pleasure.

Poe's characters consistently choose fear, for example, debilitating and distracting, rather than the soul "toned" by health. Fear is itself an object of desire. In a strange passage in "The Fall of the House of Usher," Usher explains to his guest what most disturbs him:

> "I dread the events of the future, not in themselves, but in their results. I shudder at the thought of any, even the most trivial, incident, which may operate upon this intolerable agitation of soul. I have, indeed, no abhorrence of danger, except in its absolute effect – in terror. In this unnerved – in this pitiable condition – I feel that the period will sooner or later arrive when I must abandon life and reason together, in some struggle with the grim phantasm, FEAR." (322)

The most important consequence of any of the possible events that might befall Usher is his experience of horror, fear, terror. It is not, significantly, death that he dreads.[3] His physical affliction, moreover, makes him peculiarly vulnerable to what he dreads: he is hypersensitive to any stimulation so that the slightest disturbance can produce the "intolerable agitation." It is a "family evil," he says, the phrase suggesting that whatever bad gene he inherited has been augmented by that other family evil, incest. Just as the infant's body is handled freely by familial caretakers, aroused to "unpleasure" by thoughtless love, Roderick has been bred to respond as he does, to be excited by things that healthier people would not notice. A genetic and cultural script has been engraved in him that emerges with each excitation. He *is* largely this propensity. And despite his special diet, clothing, and music (322), his actions throughout the tale are calculated to reproduce this agitation. Pain and dread, it appears, are no impediment to his pursuit of the effect. Specifically, he buries, with the narrator's complicity, his living sister.

It is doubtless correct to see this burial as a repression of an illegitimate desire. But I want to focus on the fact of his burying her where he (and the narrator?) will hear her inevitable struggles to escape. The effect on him of Madeline's illness is to heighten his

53

artistic production: his painting, music, and poetry all take on an intensity that leaves the narrator shuddering "thrillingly." And once Madeline has been entombed within the house, Roderick's attention becomes wholly focused on something that the narrator claims not to understand, but to be "infected" by (330), so that he too is aroused, focused, sleepless. Burying Madeline has done nothing to return Roderick to anything like a sense of calm, and it has led the narrator into a fuller participation in Roderick's situation.

When Roderick finally collapses beneath Madeline in their parody of sexual embrace, the narrator comments that Roderick fell, "a victim to the terrors he had anticipated" (335), not a victim of Madeline's desperate clutch or vengeance. The terror was not only anticipated, but prepared – but what exactly is it? The clutch between Roderick and Madeline does not produce a literal union any more than a sexual encounter would. Although incest is in the air, incest is impossible. Rather, it represents a displaced desire for some more fundamental union, more extreme, more dissolving than a mere sexual union could be. Kristeva argues that horror is evoked by those things that recall too clearly the role of the body and *jouissance* in the making of the individual. The washing, rocking, suckling, and murmuring, together with all their odors, bind the infant's body to life through the mother's body. (Some newborns, if not aroused to eat, would calmly starve to death: "fail to thrive," we say.) Kristeva's "horror" recalls, specifically, this mother–child dyad, which culture requires be dissolved for the business of being human to proceed but which always threatens to return (1982: 64). Within Kristeva's model, the symbolic world that we normally inhabit with its usual desires and satisfactions floats on the body's memory of these early excitations (the "semiotic"), so that the excitations retain a place in the complex of displacements that constitute culture. The pleasures symbolic life recalls are not the enjoyments of the dyad, those sought by an Oedipus longing obsessively for a lost home ruled securely by the phallic mother. The oedipal, in fact, screens those semiotic enjoyments by interpreting all pleasure as the satisfaction of desire, an interpretation that consigns the subject to doing culture's work by pursuing the sublimating pleasures it offers.

But the memory of those early arousals of the polymorphous perverse body are not lost, as Kristeva claims and I think Poe shows us. Neither are they, however, open to conscious reexperience, for exposed to the vigilance of "lofty reason on her throne," they would be denied. The "dyad," as Kristeva imagines it, represents a condition without relation: no hierarchy, no priority, no differential structure: a "singularity," to borrow from the language of black holes (Hawking 88). The oedipal is the shift into "relation" – and hence the move into meaning and reason – a condition that the Imp of the Perverse denies. The two conditions are neither oppositional nor exclusive but exist in separate realms of unconsciousness: the dyad in the unconscious *preceding* symbolic awareness, the oedipal union in the unconscious *closed off* from consciousness by repression. With regard to semiotic enjoyment, then, reason's function is not to prevent what is repressed from irrupting into consciousness or behavior but to protect from consciousness what might otherwise be destroyed so that it can continue to provide pleasure, even if that pleasure is experienced as horror.

Roderick's stated reason for not placing Madeline in the distant cemetery is that certain "medical men" had taken too great an interest in Madeline and, presumably, might dig her up. I think we can take him at his word here, for it is clearly crucial that doctors not look too closely at his loved one if he is to preserve Madeline as a "living dead." She is kept where his "family evil," his hypersensitivity, grants him privileged access to her. The several equations drawn in the story between Roderick and the house he inhabits let us say almost literally that Roderick has "engraved" Madeline in his body, as torture and pleasure. He had no intention of ridding himself of her.

This burying of his sister seems to literalize an "engraving" that occurred much earlier. The narrator's ignorance of Madeline's existence in the family of his close boyhood friend suggests that Roderick had from childhood felt the necessity of hiding her. As the end and embodiment of his family line, Roderick would find his bliss through the exercise of that which most specifically characterizes him, the family trait. This trait *is* his sister, his twin who would have been part of his earliest physical and psychical life, and whose name, Madeline, overlaps with the designation of nervous excitement as "malady." Add to this repetition the near homonym of "m'lady," and "the lady Madeline" ("[for so was she (always) called]") becomes the malady, the evil, the literalized family. She is the missing part that makes all of the family compounded in Roderick's genes into the family name, the "her" that makes "us" into Usher.[4] Madeline is engraved in Roderick's genes, his language, and his name, both inscribed and entombed, ever present and always hidden.

We can now see that when Roderick says he must eventually "abandon life and reason together, in some struggle with the grim phantasm, FEAR," he has recognized the alliance between life and reason, though he may not know that "fear" is the name life and reason give to a pleasure that does not acknowledge them in turn. Rationality, as an ego-preserving mechanism of the reality principle, distinguishes life from death and chooses life. The "fear" that the lady Madeline represents ignores that distinction, seeking its own satisfaction without regard for the good of the larger organism. The experience of bliss can be dangerous. In burying his sister alive, Roderick has in fact chosen to abandon life and reason. This is not an aesthetic that would endear one to the local authorities.

Cons and Diddles

In the so-called tales of ratiocination, the encounter between reason and an excessive pleasure occurs in the form of a "diddle." The show of reason in the diddler gives us – the gulls – license to abandon reason in the anticipation of an unearned pleasure. But even in a macabre tale such as "The Fall of the House of Usher," the narrator is a sort of shill, someone on the scene who enacts the rules of rational life to provide us with a standard of normal behavior. The function of the shill is to allow the gull to think he has seen through the "trick" and assume that he, no longer duped, can succeed. That is, the failings of the narrators only encourage us to apply a keener reason, a rationality superior to the tales they tell, but still in the name of pleasure.

In a situation similar to that of "Usher," the narrator of "The Gold-Bug" visits a misanthropic friend, Legrand, of dubious mental stability. The narrator's quotidian sanity and lazy skepticism provide a perspective on the story that most readers would probably share, a familiar eye on an unfamiliar subject. The story is notable for its display of analytic method, particularly in its deciphering of the coded message discovered by Legrand. And it is Legrand's ability to decipher the various codes that ultimately wins the narrator's faith.

But the solution of the mystery is not the exercise in pure analysis that we would like to see. The deciphering of the cryptograph (unscrambling the letters to produce the English text), despite methodological quibbles, is sufficiently straightforward, but it is the only part of the mystery that a reader might independently solve based on information that is given in the story. The message is still coded, and although its solution (the location of the gold) is "ingenious, simple and explicit" (594), it cannot be deduced without knowledge that Legrand alone possesses. But even if we grant Legrand's special knowledge, what remains incredible is the way the circumstances necessary to the solution come together by accident: finding the scrap of parchment, keeping it, exposing it to heat; the fortunate clue of the English pun on Kidd; the fact that this valuable piece of paper was lost by Captain Kidd after he took so much trouble to make it; or that it should have been preserved unprotected for more than a hundred years. A skeptical reader might also wonder at the use of typographical characters in the message Kidd wrote by hand. A difficulty of similar magnitude appears if we consider how it was that Kidd managed to discover the tree limb to which he nailed the skull that marked the place of the buried treasure: the limb was visible solely from the "devil's seat," but unless the skull were already in place, the location would have been invisible. A more suspicious person than the narrator might have suspected Legrand of forging the thing. The degree of coincidence and accident is beyond belief as soon as one loses faith in the storyteller, but for one unquestionable fact: the gold exists.

In an essay on "The Purloined Letter," Robert Gregory points out the mundane fact that mysteries are written to flatter the purchasing public as they "solve" the mystery. The writer's interest, that is, is gold, just as Dupin's is the rich reward. Or, as Gregory notes, Dupin wants to make some bread, *du pain,* by duping his audience. And although we should be skeptical of those who want to make money from us, it is difficult, as Legrand notes, to distinguish between desire and belief when a fortune is at stake. Under the pressure of desire, the coincidence, like the pun, seems to disclose a hidden meaning. As he listens to Legrand's detective story, the narrator is

57

"stupified" by the coincidence: "The mind struggles to establish a connexion – a sequence of cause and effect – and being unable to do so, suffers a species of paralysis" (581). In Captain Kidd's case, he ensures his wealth by effectively paralyzing his assistants in crime: "Perhaps a couple of blows with a mattock were sufficient, . . . perhaps it required a dozen – who shall tell?" Legrand admits delivering a few blows to the narrator's head, to "punish [the narrator] quietly, in my own way, by a little bit of sober mystification" (595), rendering him unconscious. Coincidence puts the rational mind to sleep, precisely because it violates the accepted standard of reality in a Cartesian world (that cause precedes effect) and promises a cheap access to knowledge, and an undeserved payoff, which is just what a con offers.

The gold bug produces the link between promised riches and the promise of an impossible enjoyment. Marc Shell's essay on this story develops the historical connection to debates over the gold standard, seeing in Legrand's absurd pursuit of gold with his scrap of paper a parody of paper money's guarantee of value (21). The capacity of paper to create wealth (which is equivalent to gold for the supporters of the gold standard) depends quite literally on one's confidence in the issuer of the note. In effect, the U.S. government plays a con game, but one so vast that no one can afford to see it collapse. The scandal of paper money, as Brian Rotman points out, is that there is no "anterior wealth waiting to be redeemed" (50). The personal wealth of each American rests on a dollar that can be redeemed only by more dollars, a situation that can be sustained so long as the fiction is supported by a faith in a governmental authority, the transcendental subject of America. The dollar, consequently, serves as a fetish to cover over the lack of this primary subject, seeming to offer the possibility of a wealth that denies the limitations of nature – "In God we trust."

But in addition to pointing to this sublime aspect of gold, the bug has a more abject set of references. Scarab beetles are scavengers, eating dung and decaying vegetation. In ancient Egypt they were associated with immortality for their connection with the cycle of the sun, whose golden ball they were imagined to roll across the heavens, and for their breeding habits. They roll balls of dung, bury them, lay eggs inside them, and the young beetles emerge (exhumed) well nourished from the ground. Life and decay (morti-fication), gold and shit are blended in the bug: the buried treasure of the scavenging (piratical) parent sustains the young. For Legrand, finding the treasure (ancient and, like the Huguenots from which Legrand descended, foreign: "There was no American money" [Poe 580]) means he can return home, back to the originating dung.

Having suffered "misfortunes" in New Orleans (gambling? finan-cial speculations?), Legrand has become a con himself, offering a vision of the stars so that his friend will continue to dig in the dirt. And although the narrator continues to look on Legrand as an unsettled intellect while he sees himself as an ordinary man, he is intrigued by the offer of some perversity sauced with "reason." The gull is always the one who thinks he can make an improbable ratio of return on his investment with only a nod to rationality, while the scavenging gold bug knows that his future depends on bullshit. And who is to say the diddled is not well paid by the pleasure of the game?

The Queen's Con

In "The Purloined Letter," the police and government as representa-tives of the law are witting accomplices to the darker pleasures of the inverted Dupin. Again, the narrator is the soul of rationality, admiring Dupin for what Dupin defines as true analysis (692). Analysis is not simply the algebraist's trust in equations, which is analogous to the Prefect's trust in some sort of equation between sign and truth, inside and outside. Rather, Dupin's method is "psy-choanalytic" or "semiotic" before its time, following displacements, inversions, negations, repressions: valuables should be hidden, so Dupin looks in the open; the writing was masculine, so he looks for a feminine hand, and so on. Or so Dupin explains to his admirer, though not to the police. Apparently, Dupin's value to the police, his reputation, requires that he make a secret of his method, en-hancing its mystery and concealing its simplicity: partisan of the queen though he claims to be, he is not above letting her sweat while he collects his money.

On the other hand, there may be less method to his work than he pretends. Lacan has pointed to the quite different code that

Dupin cracks, that of the lady spread across the room like the widely dispersed, and therefore invisible, names on a map, with the fireplace marking her genitals and her black secret (1972: 68). It is easy to see why the police might have missed this display, as literal minded as they are. What is less easy to see, as Gregory has pointed out, is why the ordinary methods of the police should have missed the letter as they worked through their Cartesian grids. Obviously they would not have. It is more reasonable to think that they did see it, but, where Dupin's discretion was not to mention it, the police's (like a good servant's) was not to notice. The Prefect makes much of the need to preserve the queen's "honor," a word that nicely divides a public appearance from an internal state of being. He is, of course, a partisan (of the queen if not of the king), a man of ideals, but it is also true that his money comes from the queen: good reason to wish her honor preserved. The word "honor" allows him to pursue both wealth and ideals without feeling like a hypocrite. That is, he must see and not see that the queen's "honor" is "lost" already in a specifically physical way. He cannot afford to see the queen represented by soiled underwear ("trumpery filigree"), a torn and dirtied letter, a large black seal where once a chaste, cherry-sized red seal had been. If he could see the queen that way, he would no longer be of use to her, nor she to him.

Dupin, however, has trouble neither recognizing the blackened queen, nor holding her honor for ransom. His opinion of the queen, despite his claims of partisanship, recognizes her dishonor. A motive for this opinion is suggested in the note left for D— in the substituted letter: "– Un dessein si funeste,/ S'il n'est digne d'Atrée, est digne de Thyeste" (Poe 698) [So disastrous a scheme, if not worthy of Atreus, is worthy of Thyestes]. The obvious sense of Dupin's substitute letter is apt enough: Dupin's switch repeats D—'s switching letters with the queen. A glance at the larger context of the familial drama in the house of Atreus, however, reveals a long succession of seductions, incest, and betrayals in which women play central roles as figures of exchange or transmission. Dupin leaves these words to let D— know that Dupin had gotten revenge for "an evil turn" D— once did him in Vienna. In a sense, what Dupin has just done to D— was to take away the woman D— thought he possessed. Only a small leap is needed to conclude that the evil turn in Vienna, a few years before the birth of the Viennese detective, involved a woman. Women, from Dupin's perspective, are all whores – "cons" in Jane Gallop's French sense (29) – a useful reduction in the present circumstances because it makes the rebus of the room legible: the queen's secret is her sex, so he looks in that spot on the room-map for evidence of her transgression, the torn letter.

Women are not in themselves very important to the reclusive Dupin, misogyny playing a large part in his misanthropy. The only person in whom he takes much interest is D—, his double, his rival, his mathematician/poet, his man/woman. Other people are so unworthy of Dupin's full extension of his talents that only D— can give him full satisfaction. The turn in Vienna seems less significant in itself than as evidence of Dupin's being out-troped by D—: Dupin simply had to turn a bigger con with the greater woman.

There is, then, in Dupin much of the "*monstrum horrendum,* an unprincipled man of genius" (697) he sees in D— and evidently condemns, although such monstrosity is the source of his greatest pleasure. Dupin's monstrosity is fully interwoven, however, with the forms of law, patriotism, and reason that surround him. The authority of the Prefect of police is built on an idea of honor, both that of the police and that of the queen he is pledged to defend. And honor is one of those qualities that ideally exclude all middle states: one cannot be mostly honorable, even though the reality of experience would seem to indicate otherwise. It is not only that the police could not see the queen as a sexual being, for they would see that fact soon enough if their reward lay in finding her guilty. What they would reject is the idea that the queen, as a token of exchange, could be both worthless and valuable, authoritative and empty. The effective inability of the Prefect to perceive this limitation of honor (no matter how willing he is to profit by it) produces the situations that allow those like D— and Dupin to act out their desires. It is finally neither the money nor the honor that appeals to Dupin, but the diddle.

The diddle is, of course, a central part of the story Dupin tells to the narrator, though he doesn't mention the pleasure. In Dupin's account, the entire enterprise was an exercise in analysis, turning D—'s trick on its head and repeating it, with a brief concession to the pleasure of revenge at the end. But the function of women remains unmentioned, although touched upon at every step in the analytic tale. The narrator's admiration for Dupin's talent presses Dupin to go over the details, to let him also understand every step, each displacement, each motivation. This detailed series of causes and effects is so neatly closed that no other explanation is necessary, so Dupin need never acknowledge, or even consciously recognize, that his deeper motivations are derived from diddling D— through the queen. In "Diddling Considered as One of the Exact Sciences," the second ingredient of the diddle is "interest": "He scorns to diddle for the mere *sake* of the diddle. He has an object in view – his pocket – and yours." So the rationale seems clear: Dupin must profit. But the ultimate ingredient of the diddle is "grin":

> He grins . . . at night in his own closet, and altogether for his own private entertainment. He goes home. He locks his door. He divests himself of his clothes. He puts out his candle. He gets into bed. He places his head upon the pillow. All this done, and your diddler *grins*. (609)

Clearly, the diddler can enjoy himself in bed, even alone. Like Legrand, he needs some law – profit – to justify his actions, but in the end he diddles for pleasure. He makes people take him for what he is not, he vexes his soul, he loses himself; and his gull, who merely sleeps in his bed and feels nothing but money when he puts his hand in his pocket, is fascinated. Dupin, the queen's repo man, will get her letter back, but not merely for the payday. He plays a royal *con* for a payoff in enjoyment that ordinary people dare only read about.

The Big Bang

It reassures us to think that Poe, even now, takes our money, that his interest is profit, which we all understand, and not simply perversity. The blinding gold justifies many plots while it conceals the drives that would interfere with our commitment to reality. Money, as desire, is a perfect figure of the oedipal phallus, mediating between loss and satisfaction, providing liquidity to sustain modern time's promising flow. Perhaps we pay to be diddled in fiction because it suggests that our being diddled in reality is only another game. But what if Poe doesn't take our money, or takes it only as an excuse, not a reason, to diddle? How do we understand an inverted world of causes and effects where the joy of diddling, not cash, structures the game, where wealth, security, and control are only the hush money paid to make us silent accomplices? Money, fame, family, and genital sex are reductions that let us control and reduce stimulation, become ordinary fucking people living under the limitations of castration, seeking merrily or gloomily whatever satisfactions we can get. If these reasonable strategies fail, we are threatened with a return to some earlier fixation with its overwhelming horror and excitement. And so we keep the diddle going, even though the plot may be made by a pervert.

One of the most elaborate diddles in Poe's writing is "Eureka." In calling this "Poem" a diddle, I imply that despite Poe's sincere preface, there is a certain "grin" to be gained by the willingness of readers to grant Poe's authority, not as a scientist (though the science is in fact fairly good) but as a writer. For the essay is, after all, not only about the universe but about the process of composition as well (Rowe 1982: 96). "Eureka" is ostensibly about the attempt to comprehend what is fundamentally unrepresentable: the origin, infinity, spirit, intuition. The "blundering ratiocination" (Poe 1274) of ordinary thinking – such as the deductive and inductive alternatives of the Ram and Hog, Aristotle and Bacon – must be replaced by a more subtle method if the entire universe is to be imagined. The fundamental problem is that thinking of the origin and end of the universe leads inevitably to conceptions that are precisely "singular," whereas between those extremities lies the universe of "relation," difference. And we are once more the cooperative side-kicks nodding our heads at Dupin's high reason.

Origin and end lie necessarily beyond the limits of the essay's discourse, entombed in black holes behind a wall the living and rational cannot penetrate – in the singularity that preceded the Big Bang, in the darkness preceding consciousness and following death, in the queen's promising, empty *con*. "*Unity. This* lost parent" (1287), he calls that beyond, whose existence he deduces from the evidence of the effects: the thinking beings we are. And confined to this world of effects, of signs, we can never in life know causes, signifieds, face to face. The lost parent is there, and will return at last, but lies buried for the *time being* in the family plot.

Poe's logic, mimicking his universe, produces movement, an end-less back and forth, an oscillation that heats the imagination without the hope of ever generating a resolution. Rational language both produces and limits this excitation, protecting and preserving "this lost parent" that is its ostensible goal. Unlike the imperfect family plot where the bodies of parents merely rot, the crypt of "Eureka" houses the living dead, the parents who are dead, but who do not know it, whose will ignores the passage of time. Poe has some curious things to say about plots. In divine creation, there is a "*mutuality* of adaptation," which means that "we may take at any time a cause for an effect, or the converse – so that we can never absolutely decide which is which" (1341). He has already established (1340) that space and time are the same thing, and it is only a matter of human perspective that makes us see cause and effect (time) as irreversible. Within the plot constructed by the divine, one could move back and forth through infinity: "The plots of God are perfect. The Universe is a plot of God" (1342).

What we have in "Eureka" is an attempt to substitute the plot of God for the family plot. All the pragmatics of reason are employed to avoid an end, the cycling movement evading the irreversible forward movement of familial production wherein the rotting of parents announces our own end. But in the end they are the same story. It is not exactly death that Poe's logic avoids: it is stillness, the loss of the "Heart Divine" (1356) that "throbs" from unity to relation and back again. When near the end of the essay he moves toward the seeming resolution of "Life – Life – Life within Life," it is not a life opposed to death, nor even a transcendent synthesis of life and death into a higher unity. He has, so long as we retain the logical paradigm he cannot jettison, performed the typical Christian inver-sion of calling death life, which means the structure remains intact, and unity–relation, being–nonbeing can continue to oscillate.

There is, Poe claims, a privileged time when such oscillation is not necessary to the feeling of Life. "*During our Youth,*" he writes, Platonic memories of Life haunt us: "So long as Youth endures, the feeling *that we exist,* is the most natural of all feelings" (1356). This "true dream" is lost to the "conventional World-Reason" of adulthood. In a Freudian age, we might also call this reason "reality": we begin to understand that we will die and begin to value life. The next page makes it clear that this dream of youth is based on pleasure, this being the connection between us and the Divine Being, who "feels his life through an infinity of imperfect pleasures" (those of mortals) (1358). Of course, youth is not a time of unmitigated pleasure or joy, though it is one of intense feeling. What Poe seems to recall is a time when this intensity of feeling makes no distinction between life and death, when an access of either joy or grief can lead to death, when a "reality principle," World-Reason, does not yet sufficiently protect the organism to ensure its survival and reproduction.

This Divine Being resembles what Lacan calls *jouissance*. *Jouissance*, which he argues has been the mystics' approach to God, is outside the structures of meaning, of *signifiance*, yet linked to them in practical life: "the motive of this being of *signifiance* lies in *jouissance, jouissance* of the body" (1982: 142). This is not a "phallic pleasure," which always means something, but the polymorphous perverse pleasure of a body not limited by the genital reduction. The ecstasy the body can produce provides a motive that the rational mind has no access to. The "memories" of divine life that Poe refers to are the product of the body before pleasure is trained by reason, and the pleasures and griefs youth finds worth dying for subsist as the motives for a rational discourse long after they can be evoked directly. That enjoyment is recalled, though indirectly, as an "infinity of imperfect pleasures," pleasure of the kind Poe can still experience. But "infinity" is a key word in this essay: "I cannot conceive infinity" (1274). It is the impossibility of conception that sustains the pleasure and pain of Poe's discourse. Conception would interrupt the plot and produce the merely family movement. The throbbing heart of life would have to be pulled from beneath the floor boards and released into the life of generations.

Stephen Hawking describes a universe that is finite yet unbounded by space or time, which he opposes to the model of a universe that must be either finite and bounded or infinite and unbounded (115ff). The finite, bounded universe must either expand forever or oscillate between black holes of beginnings and ends, expanding and contracting in the interval. The fate of

Hawking's universe is less clear. It requires no beginning or end, hence no Divine Being, no spark to initiate the laws of creation. There are an infinite number of possible histories of the universe of which the one we inhabit is only one, which implies the impossibility of ever attaining a perfect knowledge of the universe. To paraphrase Lacan, "L'univers n'existe pas." [5] If Hawking is right, no superconducting supercollider will ever let us finally know the Big Bang. A clear vision of the beginning of the cosmos is as delusional a goal as is that of the perfect sexual union, the ecstatic dissolve of bodies that haunts love. Rather, we are left, happily enough, within the realm of "imperfect pleasures."

The discourse of science by which Poe attempts to define a universe clearly structured by big bangs comes up against a universe that resists the dream of "perfect pleasure," the stumbling block of ordinary fucking people, those who hope that knowledge and sex will lead toward satisfying wholeness rather than the brute fact of an unassimilable Real. We are, as individuals, as Americans within a community, each of us possessed by a hard kernel that separates us not only from one another but from ourselves, a mystery as terrible as it is thrilling. Larry Vaughn, thinking about what remains incalculable in Poe's mysteries, suggests what most other writing lacks: "In the reification, the forgetting, of that which lies outside the narrow domain of calculation, namely human suffering, thought loses the negation and resistance which first constitutes it as thought, it devolves into the affirmation of existent realities and becomes thoughtless" (98). Poe's writing, however, never forgets the human body of suffering and pleasure that denies the reduction to a unified whole, a singularity. The black hole – the dream of an origin and the promise of a return – is a con, a game that lets us take the illusion of authority for the source of truth, take the queen's – the mother's – genitals for the source of sublime happiness. What Poe ultimately offers us instead is the infinite imperfect, the repo man's anxiety, the perverse pleasure of what ultimately will not submit to the control of perfect ownership, of mastery, of death.

4

"TOO RESURGENT"

LIQUIDITY AND CONSUMPTION IN HENRY JAMES

—————

> "Women were thus endlessly absorbent,
> and to deal with them was to walk on
> water."
>
> *The Ambassadors* (322)

In the American popular imagination, to be a scholar, someone dedicated to textual knowledge, is to be "dry as dust," as if professional readers have a problem with pleasure. Academic scholars' interests seem narrow, arcane, and, as even my colleagues in the professional schools tell me when the question of salary arises, worthless. Scholars do not participate properly in the joys and profits of ordinary people, taking too much interest, like several of Poe's heroes, in paper. However, when popular culture does show an interest in academics (as in a television drama, for instance), it suggests in a curious reversal a different problem with pleasure: it is not that scholars enjoy no pleasure, but that they enjoy too much, and in the wrong place. That is, some people, the bookish, choose to disregard the presumed pleasures of a normal life with its mundane violence, greed, and sexual hydraulics for the "smothered rapture" available to the "intellectual nostril," as Henry James puts it so suggestively.[1] Occasionally, the sources of rapture are represented as sublime and the text worker as an uplifter of children and lover to sensitive women. At other times, the sources are abject and the scholar is perverse. In either case, such readers' pleasures are disturbing because they sniff at some limit in conventional expressions of healthy sexuality, a flaw suggesting something so unsatisfying in its pleasures that a whole class of people would turn their backs on it.

Curiously, literary scholars seem to dislike the bookish sniffer as much as or more than common readers do, perhaps because they spend so much time with them, as them. Tony Tanner writes with distaste of the prying narrator in James's "The Aspern Papers," claiming "he has wasted, and degraded, his normal sexual instincts into a lascivious lust for paper" (22). This seems strong coming from a man who has also devoted his life to paper, but advocates of "normal sexual instincts" are often repulsed by the supposed enjoyments of the "abnormal," as if contamination endangered them. Some paper is clean, it seems, while other paper is filthy, but how do you tell the difference? Seeking some encouraging sign of health in this same story, Donna Przybylowicz looks to Tita's final burning of the papers Aspern left behind. There, after years of cloistered emptiness, Tita can "begin to experience the fullness of life and the present" (156).[2] According to this reading, although the narrator may have wasted his own life by not having taken up Tita's offer of love and marriage, Tita – old, poor, alone – at least has a healthy outlook and a grip on reality.

There is a problem with what James's characters want, particularly when they want neither love nor money, and so we see Maisie, Isabel, Strether, and others as having "renounced" what seems desirable. Carren Kaston devotes a book to discovering the positive side of renunciation: whereas it might seem that renunciation is an expression of the character's (or author's) castration, Kaston says, by the later novels, renunciation has become a step toward the development of an independent imagination based on openness rather than exclusion. And so although poor old Strether does not enjoy the pleasures of Paris, neither does he settle for the dreary financial security of Woollett's productive factories; rather, he looks to some more open, if indefinable, existence. The concept of renunciation, however, retains the idea that something desirable has been sacrificed, abandoned for a higher health – but what does Strether renounce? Although he is infatuated with the city and lives out half of an idyllic fantasy during his walk in the countryside (until it runs up against reality), Paris reminds him in the end of what he has lost: his wife, his child, his youth. A marriage to Maria Gostrey would seal his fate: she wants simply to care for him as he drifts into old age and death, a prospect Strether may not relish any more than that of dying with Mrs. Newsome. Perhaps for Strether there is nothing to renounce.

By comparison, the narrator of "The Aspern Papers" may have even less to renounce. I have heard enough men, young and old, laugh vulgarly along with the narrator of "The Aspern Papers" at the absurdity of marrying a ridiculous old woman like Tita Bordereau, but I suspect age is not really the issue. Eve Kosofsky Sedgwick's analysis of James makes the interesting argument that some objects of desire may be forgone because they are, simply, not desirable (164): a homosexual man does not "renounce" the pleasures of a wife's bed. The problem with marrying Tita, as Sedgwick suggests, would be that the narrator wants something else, but something he will not recognize. For many people, their objects of desire may be obscure, but at least they can be represented by money, a spouse, commodities, and other pleasing shapes with which the modern world rewards us for doing its work. Consequently, although the source of each person's real enjoyment in work may lie hidden, these rewards provide a cover story to conceal that enjoyment, a story more socially acceptable than "renunciation." For others, the cover story merely reveals some other, perverse enjoyment. Perhaps the narrator of "The Aspern Papers" elicits the reproach of Tanner and others because, like the scholar, he pursues a task that begins, at the dawn of consumer culture, to betray those other ends. In this story and others, James reveals something about the way our culture does the work of reproducing itself.

In "The Aspern Papers," the high cultural business of maintaining the reputation of a sublime poet comes up against the low culture of cash and the fact of bodily presence. When faced with this conflict, the critic retreats to the cloister of his office to preserve the poet. In *The Ambassadors,* the sudden rush of cash and bodies into the scene destroys the cloister of family business Strether had inhabited. At the same time, Chad Newsome begins to establish a new fantasy based not on the sublime of high culture – as embodied in Madame de Vionnet's taste, family, furniture, and title – but on the new science of advertising. These two stories of the emergence of new social conditions will help clarify the way perverse enjoyments can undermine cultural projects or be employed to do the work of social development.

Here is one possible paraphrase of "The Aspern Papers." The narrator has dedicated his life as an editor and biographer to the textual capture of the dead poet Jeffery Aspern, apparently excluding more normal joys. When he discovers that the Romantic poet's muse and one-time lover is still alive in Venice and holding many of Aspern's unpublished papers, he plots to ingratiate himself with Juliana and Tita Bordereau (Aspern's lover and [some think[3]] his child): he rents a room in their house at an exorbitant rate and floods them with flowers. Not only does he pay more than the room is worth, but he pays more than the papers of his god would be worth on the market, revealing to the Bordereaus, as well as to us, an excess in his desires. He wants not only something he will not disclose to the Bordereaus but something he cannot articulate even to himself. The Bordereaus, although they do not understand him, see through his design and humor him. The Misses Bordereau despise the prying that accompanies literary biography, but they also see the editor as a financial and matrimonial prospect and take much of his money. Just when he thinks he will achieve success, the price that the man is apparently asked to pay (what the Boarder owes) for the papers is marriage. He refuses, the younger woman burns the papers, and the narrator settles for a lifetime of "chagrin."

Or so he claims. If it were simply that his passion for Aspern allowed no room for another love, he would at least know what he wanted. But his behavior seems to guarantee that he will miss an encounter with the man[4]: he protects his god Aspern from critical, historical analysis by confining him to the negative space of the missing papers. Rather than see Aspern's sins and failures and acknowledge the human limitations of the great man, he preserves the image of the sublime, unreachable poet, denying not only Aspern's ordinary pleasures and sexuality but his own as well. As a consequence, he has developed the finicky, arrested impotence that makes him so unappealing to most readers. But if his desires were truly so constrained, he would not be the easy mark he is for Juliana, who sees that he desperately wants something. He is, I think, bound to another kind of passion that appears persistently throughout the story, one that points to a more perverse attachment to Aspern. We see this pattern in the signs of liquid presence to which he is drawn but that threaten to engulf him.

The Bordereaus, as their name says, are the liquid edge, the border of bodily presence.[5] Their water-cut city, the humid air, and their damp summer garden in which the narrator frequently sits seem to offer something distinctly different from dusty paper and bones. Even the very old woman, Juliana, is "too resurgent" where the narrator had expected to find only a desiccated reminder, a left-over piece of the absent Aspern. What these women offer is not, after all, the truth of the man but the insistence of female bodies, not signs but some unmanageable reality.

The narrator's relation to Aspern is from the beginning of the story marked by ambivalence. He loves the poems but has trouble reconciling the reputation of the man with his writings: Aspern's relations with women were alleged to be "shabby." The narrator euphemistically notes the story that Aspern had "treated Juliana badly" and "'served,' as the London populace says, several other ladies in the same way," but one of his major scholarly accomplishments had been to clear his "god" of that charge (James 1962: 156). The narrator has passionately devoted his own apparently celibate life to Aspern's, but only by denying the conventional excesses of bodily pleasure that marked Aspern's life. The value of the poetry for the narrator, that is, does not lie in the record of physical pleasures the poems provide but in the translation of a divine Juliana into an even more divine poetry. His passionate interest in the letters themselves, however, betrays a different locus of his enjoyment.

Tony Tanner writes of James's own relation to the pleasure and romance of Venice: "The name permanently pre-empts the place and . . . the word finally pre-empts the name" (5). The city, like the lover, is ultimately a matter of language for the writer, not simply in its function as a signifier but, to Tanner's disgust, as the word itself. This perversion of language interferes with the "normal" pleasures of the city and, for the narrator, the normal pleasures of women. Venice, as a "site of semantic excess" (5), leads writers astray; and the signs, so much richer than any reality they might refer to, lead the devoted reader astray, promising enjoyments that leave him unsuited to the ordinary pleasures of the city. Carl Maves, commenting on James's fascination with the romance of Italy, notes that "the romantic emotion is primarily a matter of self-deception," and that Venice is the most romantic, hence most deceptive, of cities (89). This pleasurable deception, he suggests, is what attracted James to Venice, and it also tells us something about Aspern the Romantic poet. He must also have loved deception and doubtless found it in Juliana, a woman who knows what love is worth. Scholarship, poetry, love, even tourism are all, when it comes to Venice, troubled by the appeal of some exciting excess, something sublime; or is it abject? What romantic fool or pervert would let himself be caught up by this ungovernable remnant, forgetting life and reason?

Juliana's interest in the letters resembles, in fact, the narrator's, but from a less evidently perverse position. She is a depressive, as we can surmise from her years of pleasureless solitude. Julia Kristeva describes depression as a defense against the anguish of a loss so central that meaning ceases to hold. People normally respond to loss by negation: we substitute signs for objects, the move by which most of us abandon the unstable world of things and lean on the more dependable symbolic dimension of language. The depressive, however, like the pervert, disavows negation, that is, denies that the loss is real and that the enjoyment of the lost person or object is gone forever. Both depressives and perverts are unable, consequently, to take pleasure in the symbolic compensation, the currency backed by one's faith that the paternal function will eventually make everything right again (1989: 43). While the pervert finds a fetish to take the place of the lost object, the depressive, Kristeva says, makes her affect itself an "ambiguous source of pleasure" (48). That is, the depressive cuts herself off from the normal world of signification in which she would have to face the loss of some great pleasure in order to preserve the lost object. In Juliana's case, the cut was prompted by the loss of Aspern. During her years of depressive labor, she has become a student of disavowal and sees in the narrator a like mind.

Jean Clavreul has noted that perverts are the only ones who know what they want: some situation reliably provides their pleasure (216). But even more than the normal or neurotic subject, they depend on the rigor of the laws, taboos, and requirements of normal social life, for these conventions define their relation to the object or behavior they fetishize. They are acutely aware of the rules governing sexuality, gender roles, and other social codes that define a normal and healthy life, for these codes constitute the stage upon which the perverse drama is reenacted. Indeed, the exclusion of the perverse enjoyment from normal overt behavior preserves this enjoyment from the dissipation and changes that accompany a too-often repeated pleasure, as well as from the disruptions to enjoyment that would come from external criticism and analysis. The perverse structure acts as a safe that, like Poe's crypts, preserves and protects the subject's access to "lost" pleasure. To some extent, then, the pervert must remain ignorant of the source of pleasure in order to retain it. For *Aspern's* narrator, however, this ignorance of his dependence on the papers themselves for his enjoyment leaves him open to Juliana's confidence game. She will offer him what he could not consciously have hoped for.

In the scholar's imagination, Juliana, although still alive, should nevertheless be text, parchment skin covering a cool, dry skull, showing none of the slick, wet signs of what must by now be ancient, forgotten pleasures. Anticipating such a creature, he looks forward to his first meeting with her, thinking he will look through her eyes into Aspern's. But her eyes are shielded and she, "too literally resurgent," has her own disturbingly physical presence. He had not expected a woman.

Their meeting has another quality that bothers him. He had expected to pay the women rent, even to pay them beyond what the rooms in their villa would be worth, but Juliana demands astonishing sums, appalling him with her avarice. Of course everyone needs money to live, and the narrator frequently mentions his own meager wealth, but there is an excess in Juliana's desire. It gets on his nerves that "the pecuniary question" (James 1962: 175) should so frequently be tied to Aspern. The question is one of value, and to have to think about it makes the contradictions in the biographer's evaluation of Aspern too evident: the divine poet is beyond mere monetary price, and yet his papers have a readily calculable exchange value. Juliana is, it appears, ready to liquidate her Aspern assets, but her demands for money exceed the editor's measure,

73

tainting him with the pecuniary flow. He finds that he will pay not only more than the rooms are worth but more than the papers are worth. Knowing what something is worth protects us against having to measure our desires: we pay according to what the market demands, not according to our psychic needs and fantasies.[6] Although the narrator would like to relegate the question of money to a matter of simple vulgarity, his willingness to pay too much reveals the excessiveness of his own desire. He had thought he wanted some curious papers, valuable on the literary market, but he was evidently paying for something more, something unspoken.

The calculations of capitalist institutions depend on our deferring the use and pleasure of objects by transforming them into signifiers. Money, especially, should not be an object, should not be poured over the bed in a golden shower, but invested, inserted into the world where it can convert all it touches into a productive round of exchangeable signs, into commodities. Our investment in circulation compensates us for the distance that inevitably opens between us and the fallen world of things, as Don DeLillo calls it, replacing belief with a circle of credit that includes us as one more valuable thing.[7] Linguistic theory shows its debt to economic theory in the way both acknowledge the emptiness of the signifier/the dollar. Just as the exchange of signifiers brings the human subject into social being, the exchange of money (rather than its hoarding) constitutes the subject of modern wealth.[8] Money, like language, provides us with an illusory control over a world that we would otherwise find overwhelming, as adult sexuality provides us with a manageable distance from polymorphous, infantile bodies. Aspern's papers function in a similarly productive capacity for his editor, biographer, and critic. Drawn into the public world of scholarship, these texts, like money, would make more text – and even make money. They protect the narrator from the abject longing he might otherwise feel in relation to the overpowering poet, allowing him to fill the socially approved role of preserving dead fathers.

It is in this context that he expects the women also to function as signifiers of the dead man. He says of Juliana, "Her presence seemed somehow to contain his, and I felt nearer to him at that first moment of seeing her than I ever had been before or ever have been since" (167); but it is precisely Aspern's presence as word that the narrator attributes to Juliana. His idea of the feminine is that she should be both origin and preserver of the poet's linguistic presence, both cause and consequence of Aspern's pleasure, but a lost cause.[9] As an inspiration for Aspern, she was not to be a shabbily used body but a sign of something sublime, and therefore something that exists only within the textual space of the poetry. As a lingering lover of the great man, she was to be for the narrator a signifier that differed from the papers only by a matter of degree, representing Aspern, yet holding him at a distance.

The presence of a second woman in Juliana's home at first merely makes more explicit the metaphorics by which the narrator denies the bodily presence of the women. When the narrator plans his entrance into the Bordereau house, he says that he will have to "make love" to the younger (if not young) woman in order to get at the papers. In this avowed hypocrisy, the narrator thinks of Miss Tita simply in terms of exchange: "love" equals papers, just as love equaled poetry for his Aspern. In this restaging of the poet's affair, the narrator imagines that his "making love" to Tita will once again produce the papers, produce the fame, produce the desire that Aspern's love for Juliana had produced. But this attempt to transform the woman into a paper fetish runs into trouble from the start. This woman whom he can hardly see except in terms of denial – she is "not young," "not fresh," her eyes "not bright," her hair "not dressed" (164) – probably *is* Aspern's daughter, his own flesh and blood as we say, a possibility the narrator cannot see. Ideally, the woman would be "not alive," so that like Poe's characters in "Berenice" and "Usher," he could take what he wanted from the blushing corpse.

His initial overture to the women after renting his rooms is to ask to grow flowers in their garden, which he will then give to the women. Miss Tita quickly interposes an economic problem to protect herself against the temptation of this odorous presence: "It costs too much to cultivate them; one has to have a man." He replies, "Why shouldn't I be the man? . . . I'll work without wages; or rather I'll put in a gardener" (164). When flowers for a moment threaten to make the man dirty, it becomes clear that these flowers are for him only flowers of rhetoric, part of the same signifying chain as the money he will use to buy the gardener and, when the garden is not

75

producing, the flowers themselves. Pleasure and its filth are contained by a series of displacements that allow him to speak of flowers without ever touching them. But for the inhabitants of a house that has contained, as Miss Tita says, "no pleasure" (178), the introduction of such immediate pleasure as the scent of flowers overwhelms their symbolic defenses against sensual enjoyment. The narrator himself is seduced by the garden: its "fragrant alleys," contrasting with (or is it complementing?) the "odor of the canals," provide the setting for the first intimate encounter he has with Miss Tita. "Being the man" in this dissolving bath of odors is a less clear proposition than he had imagined. Subsequently, he takes Tita out for the day in his gondola, and again the liquidity of Venice surrounds them. The "slow strokes" of the oars become "more musically liquid as [they] pass into narrow canals," eliciting "a murmur of ecstasy" (though "no high-pitched voice") from Miss Tita. The narrator meanwhile "[pours] treasures of information about Venice into her ears" as she lies back, receptive (204).

My point here is not the obvious eroticism of the narrator's descriptions but the ways in which every form of discrete, symbolic exchange is subverted by some more fluid contact, some dissolution of clear distinctions. Such a failure of the symbolic function is not what the narrator had planned, not what he had imagined to characterize the life of Aspern. Aspern, as a "god," as a genius, embodies for the narrator the ultimate triumph of language over the flows of bodies, as if poetry itself were not the manifestation of language's liquid base. And the narrator's institutionally designated function as an editor and biographer has been the establishment of clarity, of repression: the poems will represent the passion that designates the woman Juliana who loved at just this time and this place. He can imagine that he does no more in consigning the woman to a signifying space than repeat what Aspern had already done in verse.

Here is the self-deception of the Romantic imagination in its avoidance of what it believes is the merely present world. The textualizing of the woman works to protect the poet from the apparent danger posed by the liquid body – not only the woman's, but his own as well. The inevitable failure of this transformation to dry clean the woman remains unnoticed, by the narrator for instance, because the poetry is so evidently paper: the women, once "served," tend to vanish while the papers remain dry, stable. But like Madeline Usher and Berenice, the women also tend not to stay in their crypts, tend rather to reemerge – horrible, bloody, and thoroughly arousing. A sticky page always signals a failure of the symbolic.

One of the questions posed by the Misses Bordereau is just what sort of pleasure one should derive from the papers. Although the canny Juliana is willing to turn the promise of the papers into cash through the high rent she charges, for many years previously she has, as Miss Tita remarks, "lived on them" (243), as if literally drawing her life's force from her handling of the papers. And when Miss Tita suggests that the narrator might have the papers if he were willing to marry her, the word becomes flesh in a manner both appalling and, for a moment, tempting. He sees that all of his attempts to contain the women within the boundaries of text have ended with the opposite effect: the papers have been drawn into the liquid realm.

"Did she think I wanted it?" the marriage prospect asks himself, his ears red, as he floats around in his gondola. Of course, she did, and she was right, though it was beyond him consciously to desire something so opposed to, well, health. As he puts it when his gondolier advises him to eat, one of the effects of Miss Tita's proposal is that, as a prophylactic measure, he "would touch no meat" (248). Only later that night as he dreams – in the "unconscious celebration of sleep" – does his longing for the papers return, making Miss Tita's meat appear to him edible for the time being. But when he finds that the papers have been burned, he leaves Venice and retreats to his study. In an effort to reestablish the order of symbolic exchange, he sends Miss Tita some money (too much) for a miniature she gave him of Aspern, claiming to have sold it, though he keeps it on his writing desk to agonize over in private.

The miniature remains as an apotropaic object, continuously prompting the narrator's desire, but only by diverting it from the sources of engulfing pleasure. The danger of this pleasure is not, of course, that he will actually drown in some oceanic bliss but that the repression that maintains Aspern as the anchor and law of desire will be washed away. The pleasure offered by the liquidity of bodies, as by the extra-symbolic presence of the text, disavows the limitations imposed by culture, family, law – the paternal function. Liquidity, as I am calling it, is no more a property of women than of men but is rather a defensive projection onto some other, a reaction to finding that the paternal function is empty. To pursue liquid pleasures consciously would, in the narrator's case, be tantamount to a rejection of the entire enterprise of the cultural deification of poets. Such a disavowal of authority would constitute a kind of revenge against Aspern, the fantastic figure who has exclusive ownership of all the women, all satisfactions, all meanings. And it is his enjoyment of this revenge that the narrator cannot bear to acknowledge. He chooses to return the women to history and its tattered papers, and the poetry to the problematics of editing where he can fully enjoy his handling of the paper rather than endanger the sustaining fantasy that great poets had great sex.

This might suggest that I think literature – or love, for that matter – entered into with sufficient perversion, or perhaps just disregard for the symbolic function, could constitute a dangerous subversion of the dominant culture, a brave world where we no longer worship nor fear great men, no longer make love with all those extra people in the bed, no longer buy certificates of deposit but keep our money in cash or gold on the kitchen table where we can enjoy it. Sedgwick seems to suggest some resolution of this sort when she, along with May Bartram, wishes Marcher would come out of the closet and be "freed . . . to find and enjoy a sexuality of whatever sort emerged" (177). But a "free" sexuality for the speaking animal is, it seems obvious, a contradiction in terms, though we might all wish Marcher were less cruel and May Bartram less complicit. Rather, I think that James is sensitive here to an emerging shift in the status of pleasure: from something to be slipped in disguise past the repressive guardians of the law to a form of the law itself.

Jean Baudrillard writes of pleasure's having become a kind of obligation in consumer society, a "fun morality" (1988: 49). But this apparent liberation of drives to seek their satisfactions is in reality a channeling of drives. Advertising, for example, "mobilizes phantasms which block these drives" (18), binding the consumers' enjoyment to the image, the advertising text, while sending them after illusory commodities. As Stuart Ewen put it in his well-known *Cap-*

tains of Consciousness, "advertising attempted to create an alternative organization of life which would serve to channel man's desires for self, for social success, for leisure away from himself and his works, and toward a commoditized acceptance of 'Civilization' " (48). While I do not think it took "captains" to produce this effect, the fact is that consumerism has become imbued with enjoyment, and love of the advertisement itself is one of our cultural perversities, our ironically acknowledged "secret" pleasures. But this pleasure is not liberation, not *real* liquidity.

James seems to see that the appeal of the perverse, the disavowal of limitations on pleasure, might more effectively serve the ends of culture than even repression can. A liquid presence, for all its promise of freedom or immersion, remains unavailable except through the forms of the symbolic. The watery world of Venice is not a matter of the presence of the sea, but the work of the canal walls. After infancy, the sea of sound is always cut by the articulation of words we speak, write, or read. The resurgence of Juliana Bordereau is an effect of the years of constraint imposed by first one man, Aspern, and then his editor. We think for a moment that the narrator will reach out and dip his hand into reality, but as with the murderer Humbert Humbert who has only words to play with, it is only by retaining the sense of poem as paper, of woman as text, that the editor preserves words' power to evoke sublime enjoyment.

Liquidity, then, is not the truth of women nor a threat to cultural stability but one manifestation of the perverse pleasure that ultimately serves the interest of sustaining cultural institutions. A Venice that had once depended on the sea to carry the ships that brought it wealth has already by James's time become a tourist attraction, but the sea is a reminder of that ancient productivity, an odorous, humid presence that underlies the visually spectacular legacy of its wealth. Today, the massive efforts to save Venice from that same sea betray the deep ambivalence we feel toward this dissolving flux that technology has convinced us, perhaps fatally, we can live without. Venice is no longer a place of productivity but of consumption where the sea is both what is attractive and what is denied.[10]

Jean-Christophe Agnew, writing on James's "consuming vision," argues that the liquid lightness of a commodified world has led to "a progressive fragmentation of human needs" as useful objects have

79

been increasingly displaced in our desires by fantasy products. The response, he says, has been the "subordination [of these needs] to a more immediately compelling need to know, to *possess* as knowledge" (99), as if knowledge could repair enigmatic loss and end desire. But this need for knowledge is in fact a denial of the knowledge that pleasure is limited, a knowledge of castration, and we seize on sublime, "unknowable" objects in the hope of grasping the secret of lost enjoyment. The narrator of this story is likewise interested not in the production of poetry but in maintaining an object that will sustain practices of authority and economy. For the most part, we consume these cities and texts, too healthy to linger on the ungovernable scent of some liquid source, yet drawn by it. The narrator's experience was to have come too close to recognizing consciously that his editorial enterprise was governed by the undercurrent of such an unhealthy, "too resurgent" pleasure. Juliana, the old con, saw the quiver of his intellectual nostril, saw a perversity he would not acknowledge, and took him for most of what he was worth.

Advertising Men

In *The Ambassadors,* as in "The Aspern Papers," a fastidious American man meets a woman and her daughter who are in possession, it seems, of a romantic lost American. Both women are younger and more sexually appealing than the Bordereaus, and the lost man is the young, handsome Chad Newsome, not a dead poet. But the structural correspondences are striking. In the course of recapturing the man who represents the future of the family business (manufacturing, this time, because publishing has been reduced to a vanity business in *The Ambassadors*), Strether becomes entangled in the economic and sexual lives of women who seem to have access to some sublime knowledge. But *The Ambassadors* ends with a scene in which the lost man is recovered, thanks to "science": Chad will turn his romantic talents to the open fetishization of commodities through advertisement. Something new seems to be emerging in this late novel.

One of the strange things about *The Ambassadors* is that the handsome, clever, improved Chad should become so repulsive a figure at the end. As he talks to Strether about advertising in the penultimate scene, he hooks his thumbs in his vest in a parodic imitation of the successful, substantial businessman. He is, evidently, the man for the job his mother is recalling him to, but why should this make him so distasteful? William Greenslade's essay on advertising in *The Ambassadors* sees a kind of moral failing in Chad, taking a view of him that reflects James's own apparent distaste for the intrusion of economics into European culture. The idea that money would displace all other cultural values, such as those that had been embodied in Strether's fantasy of Europe, seems to have inspired a kind of dread in James, one similar to Spencer Brydon's on coming across his awfully dismembered, awfully rich double in "The Jolly Corner." But it was his education in France that allowed Chad to discover the connection between advertising and pleasure, a connection that openly shifted the nature of business from producing goods to consuming commodities, from the health of real things to representation and fantasy – at a price.

Of course advertising and capitalism were changing in the decades around the turn of the century. The success of industrial production had required the development of a consumer culture to absorb the products pouring so plentifully into the market. This success in turn required a new mode of advertising to produce a continual demand. Earlier advertisements had found it sufficient to proclaim (often in extravagant lies) the virtues of their products, believing that people would buy useful products if only they knew of them: medicine (the biggest advertiser), land, or the common household item produced in Woollett. But the new science set out to exploit a gap between need (a problematic category in any case) and desire and began to devote itself to producing "new needs" (as one telephone advertiser artlessly announced his intentions to me) rather than to providing information. The gap between need and desire had always been there, but the new ad brought with it a surprising surplus of enjoyment divorced from the pleasure of whatever product might be offered. T. J. Jackson Lears, commenting on the transformation from production to consumption, from scarcity to abundance, notes that consumption is the "therapy" provided by an economy that had deprived people of a sense of wholeness: "In the United States as elsewhere, the bourgeois ethos had enjoined perpetual work, compulsive saving, civic responsibility, and a rigid morality of self-denial. By the early twentieth century that outlook had begun to give way to a new set of values sanctioning periodic leisure, compulsive spending, apolitical passivity, and an apparently permissive (but subtly coercive) morality of individual fulfillment" (3). Even if one did not need or want the products, consumer-driven capitalism found an ally in the enjoyment afforded by fulfilling the moral command to consume, by the very process of being sold.

While James's readers mostly despise the narrator of "The Aspern Papers" – for his prying, for his perverse interest in paper, for his lack of interest in normal, let's say manly, joys – it is just such a sense of cultivated manliness that Chad appears to embody when Strether first arrives in Paris. Modest, direct, beloved of lesser men and beautiful women, but most of all a man who knows what he wants, Chad is someone who evidently understands how to avoid the mistake of not living all you can. He represents the alternative to what Strether had known in Woollett, a world governed by Mrs. Newsome's too-evident interest in the bottom line. What you *really* want is something else. Paris had long been the place to supply one version of that something else, and Jim Pocock is eager to get a look at it. But what Strether finds himself attracted to, and what Mrs. Newsome sends her daughter Sarah to put an end to, is something unhealthy.

The Paris that Chad has imagined for Strether has ceased to be productive, ceased to lead anywhere. Walter Benjamin, writing about Paris and the Arcades, remarks on the way commerce and its architecture have provided "images and wishful fantasies" that "seek both to preserve and to transfigure the inchoateness of the social product and the deficiencies in the social system of production" (148). The particular fantasies of the Arcades not only preserve an inchoate, troubling social system, but they infuse it with new energy. Benjamin continues: "The entertainment industry facilitates this by elevating people to the level of commodities. They submit to being manipulated while enjoying their alienation from themselves and others" (152). The social connection here, the community, consists of an eroticized exchange of fetishes, hardly the ideal of men working together that Emerson imagined. Maria Gostrey, the guide to this new world, has specialized in the Paris of the tourist, playing the guide to consumption, knowing all the markets and all the best prices. Her sexual proposition to Strether at the end of the book amounts to an invitation to join her in her acquisitive life until he dies in her care.

Strether notes that Paris is an "assault of images" (James 1964: 120), one consequence of which becomes evident when he attends the artist Gloriani's party. Entering that world, he has "the sense of names in the air, of ghosts at the windows, of signs and tokens, a whole range of expression, all about him too thick for prompt discrimination." And seeing his host, he finds that Gloriani's face is "like an open letter in a foreign tongue." Strether assumes that with more time and discrimination the "signs and tokens" would reveal their meaning, but until that time, they provide, like the letter in a language you can't read, a literally meaningless enjoyment. Like commodity fetishes, the signs in Gloriani's face provide an enjoyment intense enough to conceal for a time the fact that they embody no discernible value. The Paris of images supports the Paris of exchange, permitting exchange to evade rational critique.

This power of the unreadable sign suggests what Lacan toward the end of his life called the sinthome, which Žižek identifies as "a fragment of the signifier permeated with idiotic enjoyment" (1991: 128). The sinthome short-circuits the satisfaction normally experienced in the attainment of a goal and instead suffuses the "aim," the pathway to the goal, with enjoyment. The ostensible end may still be attained and produce much happiness, but the actual motive for following the pathway or script that leads to the goal may be the pathway itself and the "idiotic enjoyment" it provides. That is, the pathway evokes the sinthome, the absent *Thing* that supports a fantasy, although it can neither represent nor capture this *Thing*. For example, many people shop not only to acquire particular goods but also to reenact a shopping fantasy. The goods, worthwhile or not, justify the shopping and thereby conceal the fantasy, and the economy prospers. Gloriani is an advertisement for art, but when Strether claims he feels as if he's been penetrated by a steel shaft, by Gloriani's "terrible life," we see that the sublime is the practiced terrorism of a powerful man working to screw Strether. And Strether, a good customer, enjoys it, even though – or because – he remains dazed.

It is significant that Strether comes to Paris longing for the yellow
literary journals of the French at exactly the time in which green
journals such as the one he published in America were becoming
profitable through the use of advertising and the diversification of
their content. Eric Stanley's history of the literary magazine notes
the reluctance of literary journals at this time to be financially
successful, although the alternative had been either failure or a
continuing dependence on the patronage of some beneficent institution. The dedication to literary values assumed by such journals
produces, ironically, a kind of paper fetish, an object of intrinsic
pleasure to be held, displayed, and saved, the effect of which is to
prop up the act of reading. In much the same way, the pleasure of
sitting in the lap of the parental reader once contributed to children's entrance into literacy. For my purposes, the difference between the literary and slick magazines (and for the survival of liter-
ate culture this may be an important difference) is that the
advertised object in the literary magazine is a kind of knowledge
rather than a commodity, but both support their offer with an
"idiotic pleasure."

Because of his resistance to the idea that he might be subject to
this pleasure, Strether is particularly susceptible to advertising's
representations. Strether's fateful journey to the countryside –
where he finds that Chad's relationship with Madame de Vionnet
involves actual sex – for all its references to art (the Lambinet
painting, Maupassant's stories) has the structure of the most ordinary of responses to a tourism brochure: the painter's fiction constructs a fantasy through which Strether can, for a time, desire –
can know what he wants. But nothing in his experience of the land,
weather, or people that afternoon escapes the mediation of the
Lambinet that he could not afford to buy years ago. The "cool
special green" he looks at through an "oblong window" (James
1964: 301) – conflating the train window with the painting – suggests that of all the "lands of fancy" that have shaped his vision ("the
background of fiction, the medium of art, the nursery of letters"),
the little green window of the dollar was the most dominant. That
is, the financial transaction, the idea that at some level only money
stood between him and satisfaction, is what protects Strether from

the immediate appeal of the land, the printed word, even the dollar bill. He does not have to worry about submitting to the sheer pleasure of the senses. Finding Madame de Vionnet beneath the parasol, however, brings him back to something real.

I don't mean to imply that Madame de Vionnet is more real than, say, Maimie or Mrs. Newsome. She has, however, learned what things cost. When Strether goes to visit Madame de Vionnet, he assumes her possessions to be completely unlike those Maria Gostrey and Chad had "purchased and picked up and exchanged, sifting, selecting, comparing" (146). In their deals, they had looked for things to buy as signs of Paris, for the exchange value, whereas Strether couldn't imagine Madame de Vionnet "having sold old pieces to get 'better' ones." Her objects, he imagines, had through time and inheritance become so utterly useless that desire could no longer be attached to them, so he calls them respectable, though he lingers over the various things with a delight for which "respectability" may not be the right word. As always, Strether responds to such enjoyment by flooding the signifiers with meaning: they meant she was honorable, "new" enough to be unique, to be, well, woman herself, "whose very presence, look, voice, the mere contemporaneous *fact* of whom, from the moment it was at all presented, made a relation of mere recognition" (150). That is, her real presence vanishes into the illusion that he "recognizes" her, which is what make him so vulnerable to her story. He gets all the pleasure of the *fact* of her but sees it only as the help he gives a poor lady who has had some trouble: " 'I'll save you if I can.' " After all, she needs money, and Strether feels a spiritual demand to know "that somebody was paying something somewhere and somehow, that they were at least not all floating together on the silver stream of impunity" (315), and so he pays, but it is just so he can remain on that silver stream a while longer.

To the narrator of "The Aspern Papers," Juliana Bordereau was, to his confusion, both a confirmation of Aspern's art and an ordinary, avaricious woman. To Strether, Madame de Vionnet is, to his delight, either "natural and simple" or, conversely, "the perfection of art." She has her "wonderful . . . way of differing so from time to time without detriment to her simplicity" (318), which he seems to think is a good thing in a woman, perhaps even a necessary thing, since it meant she could "make deception right": she could lie beautifully, without the necessity of sticking to something solid. "Women were thus endlessly absorbent," he notes, "and to deal with them was to walk on water" (322), which would make any man who thought he had succeeded feel divine. But how much does it cost to feel this way? When Strether looks at how Chad has benefited from Madame de Vionnet's company, his appraisal of her talents is more exact: he says to Chad, " 'You've defined yourself better. Your value has quintupled' " (337). Like the narrator of "The Aspern Papers," Strether exaggerates all values because the true sources of enjoyment remain hidden: he loves the con.

Before Strether first went to visit Madame de Vionnet, Chad told him that she "won't do anything worse to you than make you like her" (143). That, however, is what she had done with Chad, not Strether: he is just like her, someone who makes deception right, someone who makes a living selling enjoyment in the guise of goods. Strether ultimately cannot bear the enjoyment. In conventional moral practice, the good man is one who ceases to respond unconsciously to desire and faces up to his fantasy, leaving his desire, in Žižek's terms, "purified of enjoyment" (1991: 138). The heroes of renunciation in much of James act on this model, refusing any choice that might be pleasurable: Strether wants "To be right," as he puts it to Maria Gostrey (344). To act this way is to recognize that the law of life is limitation, to keep before your eyes "the point where the death comes in" (Chad's insight into marriage vows) when you make a promise. This recognition, we imagine, provides our life some consistency, a moral imperative that preserves and defines both the possibilities for pleasure and life's discontents. Chad, however, unlike Strether, has been formed by Madame de Vionnet, "formed to please" (344).

He comes on at the end like any bloated piece of masculinity, though at the same time he is, disturbingly for Strether, more like Mrs. Newsome than his father. He tries to sound honorable about Madame de Vionnet, calculating just what he owes her and what he is willing to pay back, but he is already thinking of his advertising life back home. "It really does the thing, you know." Affects sales?

Strether suggests helpfully. "Yes – but affects it extraordinarily; really beyond what one had supposed" (339). What so delights Chad is the disjunction between the advertisement message and the sale: there is something extra to the ad, something "really" beyond the meaning, that affects behavior. That's the thing. In our present economy, I suppose we might call it "consumer confidence," by which I mean only the willingness to overlook the hysterical nature of desire and embrace the fantasy of it as your own. Chad can look at poor Strether – "depleted as if he had spent his last sou" (399) – and see the effect Madame de Vionnet has had on him, how willing he was to spend for the right illusion. She has allowed Strether to turn his life over to her, to submerge himself in an unhealthy pleasure under the alibi that he was serving duty. Chad has realized, in short, that although people need a law to believe in, what they really want is the stupid pleasure of the "nursery of letters."

Chad and Strether thus split the functions of the narrator in "The Aspern Papers," Strether remaining committed to a sublime notion of life that he cannot obtain, Chad fully displaying the fact that advertising and consumption depend on the perverse. The split allows us to find both a nostalgia for a collapsing fantasy of a life beautiful, rich, and sweet, such as that staged by Gloriani and Madame de Vionnet, and a brutally direct critique of consumer culture. But the split is only apparent: the high modernist aesthetic of Strether's art has already prepared the notion of what Baudrillard calls the "precession of simulacra," [11] a commitment to the image that disavows the limits of an underlying reality. The novel marks the point where high art and its beautiful, comforting delusions are being displaced by popular culture, where repression is replaced by perversion,[12] and Chad stands there as the thick evidence of the vulgar enjoyment – and rich profits – this change will produce. He displays the level of stupid pleasure that consumer capitalism has come to depend on, shows that the law of supply and demand is no longer (if it ever was) more than a fantasy. We are urged to consume, not for our own benefit, but for that of The Economy. (One *San Francisco Chronicle* [December 25, 1991] headline declared, "Retailers complain that shoppers bought practical items instead of splurging.") Advertising, by convincing us that our own needs are real, provides the alibi for the enjoyment we derive from the simple act of consumption. We know, but we never accept this cynical knowledge, for to live with such knowledge is to abandon the fantasy that we will find the object of desire, that we will ever know what we want.

5

ALPHABETIC PLEASURES

THE NAMES

In my telephone book I find a separate listing for "CIA," as if they understand that many people who may want to contact them know only the abbreviation. As if they know that for aspiring informers the words "Central Intelligence Agency" have for years said less about that fantastically uncentered, nearly autonomous disseminator of misinformation, paranoia, and terror than this trigrammaton: CIA. James Axton, first-person narrator of Don DeLillo's *The Names*, calls the CIA "America's myth" (317), suggesting its power to comfort and coerce as it sustains our culture. During the Cold War period, when duplicity defined the relation between communism and democracy, America needed an agency that could see through the lies of the East while it concealed America's secrets – which required its agents to lie. As Frederick Dolan argues, the CIA has mirrored the delicate balance between America's fictions of itself and its belief in a solid reality (1994: 2–3). As myth, however, the CIA transcended this instability, not through the presentation of an alternative vision (although propaganda has been a major job of the agency) but through mystery: the shadow organization stood as a sublime American presence not only in the States but also around the world. Particularly in its abbreviated form, then, the CIA's sublime, and subliminal, function was to be the One supposed to know the why and wherefore when all seemed chaos to mere citizens. Like the acronymic name of god, the tetragrammaton YHWH, the letters screen, for believers, the unspeakable name. (According to *The Cambridge Bible Commentary Edition, Exodus* 23, the letters mean "I am who I am" to the Yahwist: the name of God and the claim to Being lie hidden and preserved in the same acronym.) The inconceivable bureaucracies, corporate conglomerates, and techno-logical systems of our modern pantheon become both familiar and mysterious in their acronymic garbs.

The Names opens with James Axton commenting on his never having visited the Acropolis, the most visible and austere sign of Western civilization's first great flowering. It still evokes the classical gods – beauty, dignity, order, proportion – even while it is overrun with tourists. This "ambiguity . . . in exalted things" (3) touches the complex of desire, fear, and despair that runs through the book. This complex appears in the politics, economics, religions, and marriages of the book: because the scale of these institutions in time and size evades the grasp of any individual, they seem transcendent, filled with a meaning that we never fully understand. At the same time, they remain, like language, vulgarly physical. We make money, laws, and love with the sweat of our bodies, while the stories pro-vided by history, literature, and advertising allow us to see ourselves engaged in a larger world. In exchange for order and dignity, we agree to live in a world partly obscure to us, in exalted ambiguity.

DeLillo's metaphor for this crossing of idea and flesh is the "cult" that Axton pursues throughout the book, a group devoted to a ritual of human sacrifice. What links the cult's members to the acronymic gods is their faith in an arbitrary, alphabetic system: the initials of their victims match those of the place names where the killings occur. For the cult, the stupid coincidence of initials becomes articu-late, and the bloody brutality of the killings becomes sublime when viewed through the agency of letters: the cult members need only agree to deny the arbitrariness of the system in order to see their actions as necessary. And although the violence resulting directly from the cult's faith in its acronymic method is clearly insane, it may be only a step away from the violence flowing daily from the ABCs of contemporary business and government.

Most events in *The Names* take place around a group of foreigners in Athens: bankers, diplomats, businessmen, spies. James Axton, an insurance "risk analyst" and unwitting employee of the CIA, has given up working in the United States as a freelance ghostwriter to live in Athens near his son, the acronymic Tap (Thomas Axton Paterson), and his estranged wife, Kathryn, an amateur archaeologist. An air of witty desperation pervades these displaced people and their acquaintances, most of them just enough beyond youth to have seen failures of marriage, career, and purpose. David Keller, for example, having just married a second, much younger wife, pursues international banking as if it were commando warfare. Ann Maitland, married to a career diplomat, structures her peripatetic life through the love affairs she conducts in each of the cities she lives in. Owen Brademas, an archaeologist, has abandoned anything like an academic life, narrowing his pursuits to finding and touching strange writings in stone. Having lost touch with conventional meanings in their lives, the characters generate alternative systems to order and justify their pursuits, as if they preferred a coherent, if nonsensical, scheme over one that had failed to deliver on its promises.

Such dispersal of motivations should, one would think, lead to an attenuation of action. On the contrary, the characters fulfill their roles with an intensity that exceeds the specific needs and desires of the individual actor: Axton, for instance, succeeds as a spy in spite of himself. It is as if their actions address some unspoken or even unspeakable need that their lives of work and language – whatever it is that makes them appear as distinct individuals – know nothing of. What DeLillo explores so remarkably in this book is the complicity between the physical texture of our daily, deliberately pursued lives and the needs that persist from what I am calling a "prelinguistic" life, that infancy prior to full speech when we were already bathed in liquid talk. For it is when screens of reasonableness have evidently failed, as they have for James Axton, David Keller, and others, that we see how the work of culture is sustained by this physical texture, like the alphabetic density of words that persists when words cease to make sense. More like the cultists than they would like to believe, DeLillo's characters respond to something like alphabetic coincidences that have nothing to do with the apparent failure and nonsense of their lives.

"Abecedarians," the cultists call themselves, students of the alphabet, beginners. We were all abecedarians once, chanting our ABCs in a simple rhyme that imposes order on what is thoroughly arbitrary, tying our letters to one of our earliest songs. To sing the alphabet is to feel an order in our deepest verbal memories, and an ancient pleasure. "Something in our method finds a home in your unconscious mind. A recognition," one cultist says to Axton. He continues paradoxically: "We are working at a preverbal level, although we use words" (208). Rather than preverbal, I would say prelinguistic, by which I want to get at a use of language that functions without symbolic representation, what I refer to elsewhere as the sinthome. This unconscious "home" or origin, assuming it exists, is the brick and mortar, the absolutely familiar elements of life that are no longer touchable except through the structure of the house. Abecedarians reach toward that primal stuff of language, though alphabets take most of us only part of the way.

Julia Kristeva has attempted to describe such a primal level of language. She sees it as part of the preverbal experiences of the child's body, the rhythms of feeding, of being carried, and particularly of the mother's voice. These first mother-words would not be heard as symbols standing in for what is absent – "mommy" for the breast's comfort, "dad" for the dark stranger – but as physical presences, the real rather than cultural construct.[1] These verbal presences, however, soon become incorporated into language, the flow of the mother's voice articulated into distinct terms whose meaning is no longer present in the sound but in the reference. What Kristeva shows is that even after this incorporation into language has occurred, the prelinguistic presence, which she calls the *chora*, is not extinguished but is, rather, profoundly cloaked by those symbolic meanings, by consciousness (1986: 109). Still, the *chora* is there, powerfully evoking, perhaps even partly reproducing earlier experiences and satisfactions that are literally unthinkable. Unlike the Freudian unconscious that shunts aside what is inadmissible to conscious thought, here we have an unconscious that inhabits the body of language, a disturbing presence carrying memories of preverbal pleasures that consciousness cannot speak of.[2] This unconscious resembles the "home," the "recognition" that the cultist claims Axton finds in his method: "preverbal . . . although we use words . . . . This is a mystery."

The alphabets, by comparison, come late, both for human history and for each child – after the spoken word, after drawing, even after writing. But these highly abstract attempts to represent verbal sounds never leave behind their specific shapes: the letter "A" drawn, painted, carved on a colored block, dressed up and dancing on *Sesame Street,* is an old friend. Grouped together as words, they continue to have a physical presence, names that leap whole from the page, that earn a place on tattooed biceps: MOM, SEX, KILL. The imprint of some letters and words is so old that they come, with habit, to seem primal, a misrecognition that lets them stand for the beginning of things. Like the fetish, they seem to deny the fact that something (a penis; a mother) was missing.

When James Axton, disturbed by the seeming senselessness of a series of murders, discovers the pattern that links the victim's names to place names, he first experiences an intellectual pleasure, but the effect on him is ultimately more profound. Although he cannot explain it, he begins to recognize (or perhaps, more accurately, to misrecognize) the preverbal home the cultist spoke of. He sees himself in geography – "Jebel Amman/James Axton" – and searches newspapers for "any act that tended to isolate a person in a particular place, just so the letters matched" (250). These recognitions return him to a lost contact with the alphabetic presence of names. When the alphabet moves from song into phonetics, writing begins to oversee voice. The early articulations of speech on paper regularize and capture the voice's indeterminacies: "Here's your name, J-O-H-N, John": a hieroglyph joined to a sing-song rhyme. There is something to this early writing that exceeds the word's meaning: the mother names, and the touch of the word in the eye and ear pleases even without making sense. Later, the physical word can still evoke that first "home" of alphabet and voice but banishes it to the unconscious. After we learn to speak and write, that is, we cannot get at that home except through the words that bar our return to it. What Axton seeks in his pursuit of the cult, in looking for these alphabetic coincidences, is a method to get back to the first time of language, to circumvent reasonable thought and encounter the aural and alphabetic density of words: Axestone. Such adamantine words say that nothing is lost to time.

As risk analyst, James Axton works in the business of loss. He travels and collects information, "[f]acts on the infrastructure. Probabilities, statistics" (45). His job is made necessary by the expectation that somewhere, someone will be "killing Americans." No one in the novel thinks too clearly about why people kill Americans, about the specific political or economic offenses Americans may have committed. Andreas, a Greek associated with the foreign group (he sleeps with Ann Maitland and is perhaps a terrorist), explains at one of the dinner parties that the interests of Greece have been for years subordinated to American strategic and economic interests. But as distasteful to Greeks as this is, America is only the most recent of countries to "humiliate" Greece (235). Owen Brademas sees the problem as a more general issue: "America is the world's living myth. There's no sense of wrong when you kill an American or blame America for some local disaster. This is our function. . . ." (114). Sublime America, present everywhere, visible nowhere. What the gods have taken away, the gods can give again, so we all would prefer to think that some exalted agency has slain our young, burned our houses, and ruined our neighborhood rather than accept the mute brutishness of life and our powerlessness to make it right. America/ CIA-the-myth turns every encounter with the Real into a sign of larger purpose. This is one role that America has served in the world during much of the last century. So long as America works as myth, every loss can be recovered.

Axton's job is simply to analyze the terror that results from the consequences of America's mythic functions. The purpose of risk analysis, however, is neither to stop the terror nor to lessen the risk. Rather, for insurance companies the point is to find the "cost-effectiveness of terror" (46): without risk, there is no need for insurance. In fact, the profit of insurance companies depends on their clients' fear's being greater than the actual risk, coupled with an exaggerated faith in the insurer's capacity to cover loss: "a complex set of dependencies and fear" (114). Terrorism, consequently, is not the enemy of international, or specifically American, business, but a component of it, and a "risk analyst" is the silent partner of terrorism, without whom the meaning of terror would be incalculable, hence nonexistent.

Our society, that is, can live with violence – or rather could not survive without it – so long as it is rationalized, represented within a myth and a technology. For instance, the cybernetic model of global interests conceives of the world as a machine stabilized by balanced responses. Insurance companies and banks are part of the world-machine's governor, sensitively adjusting the forces of instability and

94

restraint to maintain the machine's alignment and hierarchies. The model also leads many to assume that proper world governance and American interests require the constant monitoring and intervention of the CIA both to promote and undermine revolutions. But DeLillo's work suggests that despite such interventions and the triumphs and griefs they produce, the agency's work is neither necessary to produce stability nor particularly effective at moving toward it. Because the interests of the groups that exert global force are so deeply involved with one another, the fact that Axton does not know that he works for the CIA along with the insurance company is less a matter of his boss Rowser's deceiving him than of his ignoring the nearly total coincidence of the two "companies'" practices and rationales.

Axton does not see and is not meant to see that insurance companies, banks, and the CIA do little to diminish the violence and chaos that blow through the nations they take under their management; that indeed they contribute to violence in an international arena – thereby increasing the risk. A simple conclusion would be that, whether through malevolence or the sheer inertia of bureaucratic growth, they sustain themselves by making themselves necessary. But I am not suggesting that the CIA of the Cold War era *failed* because it produced more enemies, more violence than it quells. I would rather turn the question, as Michel Foucault does, and ask "what is served by the failure" of the institution (1979: 272). We have difficulty comprehending nonproductive pleasures and compulsions because productivity is built into the fabric of our culture.[3] Concepts such as freedom, progress, even humanity depend at some level on productivity and its associated terms. Except when we call it art, we usually reject explicitly nonproductive activity. So rather than accept such explicitness, we mask nonproductive institutions under the guise of "failure": in a better world, the CIA would ensure peace, and universities would produce good citizens. The very concept of "failure," that is, provides a screen against recognizing drives that would otherwise have to be seen as perverse. Better not to see them at all.

Foucault's turning of the question suggests that the failures of the CIA must have some function, although not necessarily a productive one. And that function, it is almost too evident, is that the CIA allows us to participate in a covert spectacle of violence both terrible and thrilling. This is a mythic function, resembling another myth Kathryn Axton discovers. She finds that the ancient Minoans who inhabited the island she is excavating sacrificed humans to the gods of fire and earthquake. The rationale for such rituals, of course, was that they appeased the gods, diminishing the destructiveness of natural forces. The immediate, and perhaps only real effect, however, was to reproduce a violence that nature had visited on the people with a violent spectacle contained within the culture. In the circle (a broken one, as *Before the Rain* suggests: see Chapter 10) of institutional complicity with some more primal need, violence is both the cause and the effect, the excuse and the goal. One of the cultists says, "Let's face it, the most interesting thing we do is kill" (293). It is an admission our culture has trouble making.

Its being interesting, however, doesn't mean that we kill for killing's sake. The circularity of the relation just described defeats attempts to find clear causes and effects.[4] Spoken language reproduces, in spite of itself, a prelinguistic babble from which it is built, evoking the pleasure that in turn motivates speech; the CIA, in looking for the roots of conflict, provoked much of the violence that justified it. In both cases, something "interesting" occurs at the same time that it is screened from view by the self-evident (and less interesting) intentions – communication, peace – of the institutions that produce it. The cult has, perhaps too simply, decided to invert the relation, bringing the interesting to the fore.

One character comes to the romantic and quite mistaken conclusion that he can get directly at this nonlinguistic world. Volterra, a filmmaker (and Kathryn's former lover), wants to make a movie of the cult. He is a one-time *enfant terrible* of film who has dropped out of commercial filmmaking to get at something he thinks more elemental:

> "Look. You have a strong bare place. Four or five interesting and mysterious faces. A strange plot or scheme. A victim. A stalking. A murder. Pure and simple. I want to get back to that. It'll be an essay on film, on what film is, what it means. It'll be like nothing you know. Forget relationships. I want faces, land, weather." (199)

What would be left out is "relationships," the reasons, the patterns of cause and effect, the plot. What would dominate would be other kinds of patterns that belong not to representation but to what he is calling "film": "If a thing can be filmed, film is implied in the thing itself. This is where we are. The twentieth century is on *film,*" which means less that it has been recorded by the paranoid's dream of "spy satellites, microscopic scanners," and so on, than that film has become part of the modern idea of reality. We experience the world as film, know ourselves in film, in the infinitely repeatable, observable images that film has disclosed. Volterra wants a film that would leave out the organizing structure of plots that occupy, console, and distract the mind from the filmic image. He wants something he imagines as pure: he "wants the frenzy of the [helicopter] rotor wash, the terrible urgency, but soundless, totally. They kill [their victim]" (249).

Volterra's conception remains unfilmed, at least in part because its fantasy of a pure killing is "sentimental," as Axton and Del, Volterra's girlfriend, realize. Volterra dreams of something like a zero degree, a pure expression – "They remain true to themselves," Volterra says of the cultists he would film – in which death retains its existential authenticity. He can believe that something in the killings is "true" because he never discovers the code that Axton found. The cultist kills according to an alphabetic pattern: the initials of the victim coincidentally repeat the initials of the place. Passion is not a consequence of immediacy but is staged, designed to repeat some earlier event. It lies in a movement of the body, hand, and tongue tracing a form, an alphabet of arbitrary patterns that appear first within the activity of living bodies. Work, dance, writing, love, thought: the concrete features of each develop through a series of moments practiced by bodies until the learning is forgotten, as we have forgotten how we learned to talk. Volterra, the romantic, sees in the ultimate gestures something sublime, purified of relationship, while Axton sees in them an arrested moment of enjoyment.

Owen Brademas also realizes this embeddedness of the alphabet and commits himself to it. He leaves the archaeological site in Greece and goes to Mewar, India, to see a poem cut in a marble embankment. He is less interested in the reasons for the poem's

97

existence – to recount the history of Mewar – than in the letters shaped by the toil of hands:

> What was it about the letter-shapes that struck his soul with the force of a tribal mystery? The looped bands, scything curves, the sense of a sacred architecture. What did he almost understand? The mystery of alphabets, the contact with death and oneself, one's other self, all made stonebound with a mallet and chisel. (28)

On the previous page, Owen watches a woman washing clothes, beating them against the stone steps. He recalls a fisherman

> walloping an octopus on a rock to make the flesh tender. A stroke that denoted endless toil, the upthrust arm, the regulated violence of the blow. What else did it remind him of? Not something he'd seen. Something else, something he'd kept at the predawn edge. (283)

Does he recall the imagined hammer strokes with which the cult killed? The preacher of his youth who "strokes the air as he speaks, then cuts it with emphatic gestures"? The alphabet of gestures underlies the sentences of life. Ann Maitland makes a similar observation about the physical gestures that sustain life:

> [t]he women kept washing floors. It seemed to be what they did in difficult times. During the worst of the fighting they kept on washing floors. They washed floors long after the floors were clean. The uniform motions, the even streaks. Unvarying things, she saw, must have deeper value than we know. (101)

The cult and Volterra's film both appear as self-conscious perversions in the world of *The Names,* illuminating, however, in their failures to evade the religious, political, and economic systems they are enmeshed in. For DeLillo, there is no getting outside of or beyond institutions; instead, he would have us recognize the underlying unreason in "unvarying things" that runs through them. Axton's son, Tap (a too-bright nine-year-old), has such a recognition at one point as he watches TV weather news in Greek. He laughs, seeing that "the idea of forecasts, the idea of talking before a camera about the weather" was "gibberish" (189). All the gestures were familiar to him from years of watching weather reports in English, but until this moment their formulaic, often ridiculous quality had been screened by the spoken report. TV weather is, if not gibberish, less than the window on the future it pretends to be. Still, something in weather reports supports a TV channel devoted exclusively to weather – the dependably irrelevant statistics, the lines of jagged blue cool fronts and rising red mounds of warm, the weatherman's merriment. Our daily encounters with an unstable atmosphere is made more regular by the puppet-show ritual of the television. More seriously, Owen Brademas says: "Masses of people scare me. Religion. People driven by the same powerful emotion. All that reverence, awe and dread" (24). Without the blinding light of faith, that is, the movement of the masses appears as what it is, emotion evoked by patterns devoid of reason. Gibberish. Owen talks to James about the *hadj* and its culmination in Mecca with pilgrims circling the Ka'bah:

> ". . . the circuit of the Ka'bah . . . has haunted me ever since I first learned of it. The three running circuits, perhaps a hundred thousand people, a swirl of white-clad people running around the massive black cube, a whirlwind of human awe and submission. To be carried along, no gaps in the ranks, to move at a pace determined by the crowd itself, breathless, in and of them. This is what draws me to such things. Surrender. To burn away one's self in the sandstone hills. To become part of the changing wave of men, the white cities, the tents that cover the plain, the vortex in the courtyard of the Grand Mosque."
> "I thought it was one big bus jam, the *hadj*."
> "But do you see what draws me to the running?"
> "To honor God, yes, I would run."
> "There is no God," he whispered.
> "Then you can't run, you mustn't run. There's no point, is there? It's stupid and destructive." (296)

Axton clings to God, to the "point" of it all, rather than admit the attraction of the pointless running, than admit that his own kind of running has a similarly pointless appeal. The point of civilized life had seemed to be the achievement of a state of peace, satisfaction, calm. But ecstasy is not calm. Etymologically, Brademas reports, it is "a displacing, a coming out of stasis" (307). Ecstasy is being unbalanced.

In *The Names*, this ecstasy occurs in an area where speech and the prelinguistic verbal *chora* meet, in glossolalia. Owen Brademas explains that it isn't necessarily a religious experience, it is "neutral," happening to "Dallas executives," Catholics, "Christian dentists" (173). It is the brain's speechmaker producing its stuff without any allegiance to a symbolic order, without reference, and yet it is accompanied by an ecstatic if delusional sense of immediate contact with reality, of "talking freely to God," as Brademas recalls the preacher saying. In Brademas's story of his childhood encounter with this purveyor of ecstasy, the preacher moves among people for whom "[h]ardship makes the world obscure" and invites them to innocence: "He tells them they will talk as from the womb, as from the sweet soul before birth, before blood and corruption" (306). Hardship and corruption are not the lot of just the poor: TV lets us understand that the world is also obscure to wealthy Dallas executives, and the "wonder of the world" lost to them. The world that comes into focus through ecstasy, the preacher tells them, is not "scenery," but something lost within the languages we come to speak.

Language is a kind of risk insurance, a contract made with the symbolic world that offers a sort of currency in exchange for a child's lost home: though your childhood has gone up in flames, I give you these tokens in recompense. As part of the reality principle, language defers and displaces desires to safer times and situations. The losses to which life is prone, as much psychic as physical, find indemnity in the narratives that continually restructure our lives. They give us a world more dependable than the one that nature has provided, one that grants symbolic rewards on which we count for most of our pleasures. But this symbolic, still world has a "literal" dimension that glossolalia springs from, the physicality of language that flows out of and over the ecstatic: "Get wet, the preacher says. Let me hear that babbling brook." This nonlinguistic language is a source of intense pleasure for those who learn its "inverted, indivisible, *absent*" voice (307).

To some extent, this other dimension of language touches even those who don't speak in tongues. The names of places, particularly, carry powerful evocations. When Axton travels, he tells his Greek concierge a place name, a name selected not by his actual destination but by his ability to pronounce it properly. He worries that he is "tampering" with "the human faith in naming, the lifelong system of images" in his concierge's mind. The Greek man does not know these places in their stone and weather, but still they have a firm existence, Axton suspects, a world that resides in these names without any specific, experiential referents. "Could reality be phonetic, a matter of gutturals and dentals?" he asks himself (103). Charles Maitland, a career diplomat, says something similar when he complains about the changing of names on modern geopolitical maps. An old name, Persia, evokes images and dreams from his childhood: "A vast carpet of sand, a thousand turquoise mosques. A vastness, a cruel glory extending back centuries" (239). Changing the names is, for him, a "rescinding of memory" that removes a vital connection to the world. The political reasons for the changes don't matter beside the sense of loss he feels in the disappearance of that old story, not because the story itself was profound but because it was his own storied Orient. The old words babble to him.

Charles's wife, Ann, literalizes this connection of pleasure to place names. Following her husband from place to place, she sees herself disconnected from the reality Charles inhabits, from a world constituted out of the abstract diplomatic relations of his work. Instead, she constructs a private map out of the adulterous affairs she has in each city. Geography, memory, and sex are held together on a base of "sheer sense pleasure" (169), the most complex motive Ann will admit to. The specificity of countries – Kenya, Cyprus – vanishes for her, as it does for all the peripatetic characters in this book, except insofar as a line of pleasure has been cut in her mind. Like the cultists, she has replaced logical sense with the physical sense of an action that takes her out of her social role. Reference is replaced by pattern and juxtaposition – Jebel Amman / James Axton – understanding by evocation.

Axton's disregard for the referential dimension of language provides the key to seduce Janet Ruffing, the dissatisfied banker's wife who has taken up belly dancing. The inappropriateness of her pale, angular form to the dance draws Axton's attention to her body and the simple pleasure it gives her through the dance. When she finishes, she joins the drunken table, where talk has lost "sense and purpose." She and Axton enter a circle where conversation has become a "curious intimacy, a sympathetic exchange made of misunderstood remarks" (222). Axton tells Janet he wants to "really talk": "Say belly. I want to watch your lips." He wants the words to take on a solidity, become a part of the voice and mouth, shed the ordinary sense that screens language, just as the formal movements of belly dancing screen the body that they also display. Axton attempts to evoke the secret of "adolescent sex," the delight and fear in words he used when bodies were forbidden. Now, as an adult for whom bodies are no longer denied, he calls on a body of words: "Say legs. Seriously, I want you to. *Stockings.* Whisper it. The word is meant to be whispered. . . . Use *names.*" Pleasure, Axton thinks, must still be secreted in words once they are stripped of "sense and purpose." Absurdly, it works, for both Janet and readers, their arousal covered by amusement. And the fact that the seduction ends in dismal sex against an alley wall only emphasizes that the most intense pleasures lay in the words after all.

The consummation of his evening with Janet Ruffing is abstract after the concreteness of their conversation. It is just such concreteness that has led Axton to follow his wife to Greece. When he and Kathryn talk, they talk not about their relationship but about the details of their life together: "The subject of family makes conversation almost tactile. I think of hands, food, hoisted children. There's a close-up contact warmth in the names and images. Everydayness" (31). Conversation here is like Kathryn's excavation, which lets her handle artifacts she removes from the earth, the everyday objects of specific people. The relationship between James and Kathryn is made of such objects. When they argue, the particular issues referred to are insignificant compared with the specific form of the fight itself:

> The argument had resonance. It had levels, memories. It referred to other arguments, to cities, houses, rooms, those wasted lessons, our history in words. In a way, our special way, we were discussing matters close to the center of what it meant to be a couple, to share that risk and distance. The pain of separation, the fore-memory of death. (123)

It is not merely another, repressed emotion that is being displaced into the fight – although there is clearly a sexual tension to the argument – but the shape of the fight itself that they recognize and pursue, an old path of pleasure.

It is this path of the letter rather than some abstract spirit that guides *The Names*. Owen Brademas speaks of public storytellers who are interrupted by their audiences when the tellers begin "to examine methodically" the stories they've been telling: "Show us their faces, tell us what they said" (276). Later, he sits with a cultist squatting in the Indian desert who tells him: "The word in India has enormous power. Not what people mean but what they say. Intended meaning is beside the point. The word itself is all that matters" (294). When interpretation is irrelevant, what becomes important is repetition, a retracing of the word's path. The word "character," as Brademas tells Tap, means a pointed stick, a scratch on the surface, not an emanation from within. This distinction between character and internal individuality is played out when Axton is attacked by a gunman while running. He thinks at first that he has been mistaken for David Keller, the banker, but when he discovers that he himself has been working all along for the CIA, he thinks that he may in fact have been the target. The shooting could be called an error only if we think of the gunman's intention as directed toward an individual identity. But on another level there could have been no mistake because Axton and Keller have the same character, take on an "exact correspondence" that voids the question. Axton's face is not his own at that moment, but one shared with all Americans: bankers, businessmen, and spies.

In a complex pun, DeLillo points to the nonabstract nature of spirit. Tap talks to a friend, Anand, about religion, about people who wanted to learn to meditate. Anand says:

> "They wanted me to teach them how to breathe."
> "Did you know how to breathe?"
> "I didn't know how to breathe. I still don't know. What a joke. They wanted to control their alpha waves." (92)

Anand is contemptuous of this desire, a seventies fad linked to eighties biofeedback technology. But James Axton hears in this "joke" a pattern of connections. Meditation, like alpha wave production on a biofeedback monitor, is a matter of breath. He thinks of old men sitting in the dust, "lips moving to the endless name of God. The alphabet." And this dust leads to our "bones . . . made of material that came swimming across the galaxy from exploded stars" (92). "Alphabreath" is the implied pun that connects in a glosso-laliac enchantment the holy man in the dust to the Dallas executives to the child saying the ABCs. The concreteness of verbal repetition undermines the ostensible distinction between spirit and the con-crete world, since spirit has body and stone is ultimately dust.

Owen Brademas's own torment stems from a particular child-hood memory of a sublime plenitude that lay within the concrete-ness of things and their names. He tells Axton, who has sought him out in India, that when he sat in a grain bin with the cult waiting for their last victim, he recalled the story of the young priest who induced glossolalia in his childhood church. As Axton explains,

> In [Owen's] memory he was a character in a story, a colored light. The bin was perfect, containing that part of his existence, enclosing it whole. There was recompense in memories too. Recall the bewilderment and ache, the longing for a thing that's out of reach, and you can begin to repair your present condition. Owen believed that memory was the faculty of abso-lution. Men develop memories to ease their disquiet over things they did as men. The deep past is the only innocence and therefore necessary to retain. The boy in the sorghum fields, the boy learning names of animals and plants. He would recall exactingly. He would work the details of that particular day. (304)

The "cure" for the adult's "present condition" is memory, which requires a linguistic repetition of a previous moment. Owen suggests that through recall of the words he could regain an innocence, when loss and desire were more clearly, if already impossibly, de-fined. It is as if all the perversions of desire that come from the crimes and compromises of adult life might be untangled, resimpli-fied. Similarly, the preacher promises an innocence to be achieved through an older language: glossolalia recreates "talk as from the womb," a strange babbling ecstasy, "an escape from the condition of ideal balance . . . the self and its machinery obliterated" (307). Axton, listening to Brademas, feels the effect of this reenactment of the past, where the "telling had merged with the event," but only to experience along with Brademas his failure to reach the "obliterated" self. Brademas describes the speech as "beautiful in its way, inverted, indivisible, *absent*," gesturing toward a sublimity to which he was never able to give himself. He misses the perversity that could open the door to childhood's founding fantasies of wholeness.

Brademas's story returns with something closer to ecstatic possibilities in the form of a novel Tap is writing based on Brademas's life. What is immediately striking in Tap's version is the alphabetic energy of his misspellings: "gang green." While the other figures around Tap's hero, Orville Benton, reach a state of "glossylalya," "breathing words instead of air," he is unable to "yeeld" and is overwhelmed with despair and fear. Tap's language is on the border between the comforting beat of childhood voices and the world of adult rationality. The logic of plot and the running stream of story both ride upon a disconcerting murmur of obsession and repetition, distress and pleasure. At a moment when Orville Benton is struggling out of childhood, trying to find an order to replace the child's vanishing certainties, the preacher invites him to return to the babble of "childs play." In a panic, he runs from the church:

> Why couldn't he understand and speak? There was no answer that the living could give. Tongue tied! His fait was signed. He ran into the rainy distance, smaller and smaller. This was worse than a retched nightmare. It was the nightmare of real things, the fallen wonder of the world. (339)

At that moment of exclusion from the Eden of Adamic speech (Brademas recalled "the boy in the sorghum fields, the boy learning the names of plants and animals"), language has ceased to tie Tap's hero to the world of "real things," and it stands for the first time bewilderingly distant. But Tap has already begun to compensate for that loss by preserving the archaic voice ("The worldwind") within a larger tale.

This structure of loss and preservation that runs throughout the book is at the heart of the most intense joys and the most profound and insidious confusions the characters experience. Producing a cure for such confusions, finally, is not the point, whether we speak of psychoanalysis, marriage, business, or the CIA. These institutions, however, preserve simultaneously both the culture that has developed around them and the encrypted words that are our only access to a lost pleasure.[5] The best work of culture can be seen as an exfoliating of this deep obsession – the making of the Acropolis, the love that "comes down to things that happen and what we say about them." But also, and indiscriminately, it produces the worst behavior. Brademas says of the cult:

> These killings mock us. They mock our need to structure and classify, to build a system against the terror in our souls. They make the system equal to the terror. The means to contend with death has become death. (308)

He sees the cult as a demystifying parody of civilized systems. It replicates our institutions' motivations, revealing civilization's "systems against terror" to be systems, like the cult, for producing terror, and ecstasy, and death. During the period of the Cold War, when the world seemed condemned to peace by the threat of Mutually Assured Destruction, the CIA's task was largely a matter of producing the thrilling paranoia that makes life worth living: making secrets, not discovering them; unearthing enemies, terrorists, wars where they might otherwise go unnoticed and unfought. As if they were America's Roderick Usher, their music so excited our senses that good citizens, like the narrator of that tale, could not tell the difference between the living and the dead, between doing one's duty (Madeline's evident need to be interred) and tormenting the innocent (the "evidence" of death was fabricated).

Axton moves in his world as a mild-mannered skeptic, conditioned by his Canadian wife to doubt American values. But his doubt does no more than set him up, a dupe for the CIA, an institution he would prefer to condemn. He is conned in part because he resists knowing the extent to which he has already been shaped by the world he inhabits. He is, for example, a literal character, the Arabic letter *jim,* as if he were already written into words that are not his meaning; he is a tool, "Axestone"; a set of initials, Jebel Amman. His father, he notes, lives within him: a genetic sentence, a set of memories, a character "occupying" his mind. He is the words that speak of family, a list of "27 Depravities" (all conventional) that he provides for his wife to condemn him by. These, his ABCs,

106

precede his claims to a rational, individuated self and are always ready to emerge in the obsessive persistence of a prelinguistic past. They are some of the "real things" that have become nightmares in the fallen world. Unlike Tap, Axton and the others remain complicit with the languages of our institutions. But for Tap (and DeLillo), who engraves his alphabet in his own text, those nightmares are occasionally still "wonders."

6

J. G. BALLARD'S EMPIRE
OF THE SENSES

PERVERSION AND THE FAILURE OF AUTHORITY

When Charles Manson invited America's youth to kill their parents, he was not resisting authority but counseling the removal of the figures of an authority that he considered already dead. The fathers had died, but they didn't know it, as one of Freud's patients dreamed.[1] In Donald Barthelme's *The Dead Father*, the Dead Father continues to burden the roving band of children long after he has ceased to function as leader, protector, or wise man, because he does not know he is dead yet: "Dead, but still with us, still with us, but dead" (3). In the end, normally, the fathers die, fatherhood goes on, and the satisfactions the children had to put off while they awaited maturity are once more delayed, held in reserve for their own children. Manson chose, however, to deny the parental law itself and the deferral of pleasure it implies, as if to say there was never a reason to wait, that pleasure is real and present.

In his book *Running Wild*, J. G. Ballard frequently invokes Manson, an American type (like Mark Chapman, Lee Harvey Oswald, and other spectacular killers from this land[2]) to inform his story of a mass parricide. Although the story is set in Britain, Ballard's vision of the world has a distinctly American cast, ruled by icons of Hollywood film (Marilyn Monroe, Elizabeth Taylor), power (Kennedy, Reagan), and car crashes (James Dean) that have defined much of America's national and international image. Behind this image, displayed especially starkly in *The Atrocity Exhibition* (1970) and *Crash* (1973), Ballard sees an affective flaw in the heart of the late capitalist machine age: as in much writing by W. S. Burroughs, one of Ballard's most powerful influences, feeling, when it is still possible to evoke it, is tied to a perversion in entertainment, advertising, and technology, a displacement of human relationships into consumer culture and mechanical images. Familiar adult emotions appear in his books at most only in the vision of some observer such as the police psychiatrist of *Running Wild*, observers whose vision is simplistic, reductive, and judgmental. The few adults who retain a normal manner in *Empire of the Sun* (1985) likewise seem simple, even if kind, beside the relatively affectless American prisoners and the character of Jim. The satisfactions of a world that we still tend to think of as reasonable begin to fail in Ballard's books, and what in Poe might appear as a wild aberration, a violent exercise of the death drive in the pursuit of enjoyment, becomes a way of life.

What Ballard describes is a world motivated not by the interests of symbolic compensations but by perverse pleasure, in which characters find enjoyment only in submission to the demands of others' desires. In the largest sense, these demands are the product of the enlightenment and financial capital, which announce that clarity, progress, and bounty can be had if we set aside passion. Let go of your certainty that the devil rules your neighbor; do not spend every penny on one wild night, but save something to invest. A countable world is a world controlled, where every lost love will be refunded. But as Atom Egoyan's brilliant examination of domestic calculations *The Adjuster* shows, the processes of controlling the world themselves produce a surplus pleasure, available to anyone who submits to them. An insurance adjuster properly motivated finds enjoyment playing a part in a victim's loss and compensation. Censors must watch pornography. And only the agreement that everyone is merely counting, classifying, adjusting allows them all to continue. Ballard finds alibis like this at work everywhere in his empire, and his books show how they allow perversion to enter into every aspect of an enlightened world.

Empire of the Sun and *Running Wild* (1989), two later works, both depict worlds of privileged childhood, interrupted in the first novel by the stark sensuality of war and in the second by the decision of the mostly teenage children to kill their parents (and maids, butlers, drivers, and guards). In both cases, the parents' function has been rejected by the children, who see that their parents are bound to betray them, to leave them without the possibility of extending the pleasures of childhood into an imagined parenthood. Unlike the earlier books, these imply that the resulting perversions are the consequence of adult error, hence avoidable.

At the opening of *Running Wild*, all the adults in Pangbourne Village have been murdered and the children have vanished, presumed kidnapped. Pangbourne Village is a wealthy condominium development, a dozen or so houses fenced in, electronically monitored, professionally maintained by a small army of keepers. The children had been provided every opportunity to succeed, attended with kindness and consideration, and kept under nearly constant surveillance, in a pleasant, suburban version of Foucault's panopticon (1979: 195–228). The narrator, a psychiatrist hired by the police, solves the small mystery of the book: the children themselves killed the adults and fled. The narrator decides that the children in *Running Wild* had ceased to live before they murdered the adults: he speaks of the children as having been "suffocated" by the situation of care and attention to which they were subjected. There is a problem, Ballard suggests, with a life of "unlimited tolerance and understanding" because according to the narrator's analysis, such a world "erased all freedom and all trace of emotion – for emotion was never needed" (82).

However, this interpretation of the situation has a romantic element to it that avoids a more unsettling, and more common, response to a pervasive, even if benign, gaze of authority. The narrator sees the problem as a lack of freedom, claiming that the children were cut off by "overcivilization" from some engagement with the real world. He sees the children's sexual fantasies, for example, as an "escape into a more brutal and more real world of the senses" (69). The killings themselves, consequently, were "no more than a final postscript to a process of withdrawal from the external world" (81) where all meaning, he suggests, including that of life itself, had ceased to exist. The narrator's fantasy of regained freedom is belied, however, by his postscript, which describes the reemergence of the children five years later as a sort of Baader-Meinhof gang (58) whose targets are the public's parental figures. Far from withdrawing from the external world of authority and power, the children continue to live through a denial of the law, restaging the scene that has tied them most firmly to the social structure.

Foucault's analysis of the panopticon may provide one entrance to the problem posed by Pangbourne Village. The efficacy of a panopticon has less to do with the restraint of the body than with the formation of a subject. The prisoners in a panoptic structure are under constant watch, visible if not actually seen in separate rooms that emphasize the individual particularity of each, dividing each from fellow inmates while binding them to the watcher who knows them.[3] The children, of course, were allowed to interact with others, and they were cared for, treated with respect and kindness, but they were relentlessly observed, meticulously known, by their parents. The wonderful and insidious effect of such surveillance is that the panoptic subjects eventually do not have to be watched, because they finally become only what is known, find themselves nowhere but in the eyes of the watcher, identifying with the image mirrored there.

The process that Foucault describes may resemble the formation of a superego, but what is disturbing about his vision is that it makes the subject's interior redundant. The Freudian conscience arises through the internalization of the parental, divine law, which watches over not only the actions but the very wishes of the child, punishing through the agency of guilt. But while the Freudian conscience watches over internal and often unconscious aspects of the self, the Pangbourne Village children are mapped superficially, every detail of visible life recorded, so that nothing but the representable counts. The individual prisoner – or patient, student, soldier, worshipper, or lover – becomes little more than what an observer articulates. Our pollsters and marketers understand that they can predict politics and consumption in the long run by treating Americans as panopticon subjects. A canny loan officer knows you well enough from a report by TRW (the company whose national surveillance haunts your every use of credit) to decide whether to trust you with $100,000 and does not need to explore your inimitable sense of humor or taste in film, much less whether the state of your conscience will permit you to ignore a debt with impunity. J. Crew is not simply wasting money when it sends you five catalogs in a summer. And yet, something is left over, left out, when the whole landscape of the subject is mapped.

"[A] tyranny of love and care"; "choking on the nonstop diet of love and understanding" (59, 65). The narrator's claims that excessive benevolence produced a community of parricides make sense only because the book defines this parental attention and love to be a matter of watch and ward, mediated at every point by vigilant devices. In such a situation, a child's every virtue and failing are evident, open to reward or punishment, approval or neglect. But a child's need for love is never limited to what a child demands or deserves. To be loved for your virtues is no more than anyone, any stranger, might expect. You want to be loved beyond your deserts, for what is "in-you-more-than-you," to use Lacan's phrase.[4] We articulate this need when we ask vaguely to be loved "for myself," as if the true self were hidden behind some superfluous excreta, some false self. Lacan indicates something more specific, if no more readily graspable: that is, when you come into social life, take your symbolic place in the larger world, some part of you is excluded and is, therefore, lacking in the subject you become. "You" as subject is not all of you. Since we seek to find in others what we lack in ourselves, we find not the other's truth but some representation of our own lack. Parenthood implies letting children believe for a time that they are loved beyond themselves, loved for what they can never hope to make manifest, never represent. From their situation, however, the Pangbourne Village children were taught that they were nothing more than the representable, nothing beyond the image.

The Pangbourne Village children knew all about representation. They were, as I have said, constantly visible to the surveillance cameras outside the homes, whose images were delivered on cable television to every home. But the monitoring took more intrusive forms. The computers on which children did homework were linked with those of the parent, who could follow and salute each child's performance: "Well done, Jeremy!" The community was to have been the subject of a television documentary; nearly all the residents appeared in *Who's Who;* doctors vigilantly recorded the residents' mental and physical health. *Playboy* was supplied to adolescent boys so that even their sexual fantasies might be available for inspection. "[S]urveillance of the heart," one policeman calls it, thinking of the intrusion's cruelty more than of the way these methods create a heart suited to surveillance. Like the souls generated by all acts of confession, according to Foucault (1980: 58–63), the truth of the Pangbourne Village children was defined – for them as well as for the adults – by the aspects of life that could be made visible. The problem with a heart molded this way is that it is not connected to a world beyond representation.

When the children first resisted the thorough mediation of their lives, they attempted not to avoid it but to exploit it, parodying its forms while removing the overlay of meaning that justified the adults' use of media. The effect was a kind of counterhegemony, not an escape from the structures of discourse and ideology but a turning and multiplying of them. For example, the children constructed alternative histories of family life in secret journals that redefined relationships in pornographic terms of power: daughters serve as polymorphous, perverse prostitutes to the rest of the family (69). One child published a tabloid-style newspaper specializing "only in boring news" ("Egg boils in three minutes") (70), which emphasized the power of media to translate all life into their own forms. Radio Free Pangbourne broadcast silence intercut with a few random sounds and breathing. A parodic documentary "adopts the style of a real-estate developer's promotional video" to record the minutiae of daily life, interspersed with television scenes of car crashes, executions, and concentration camps. There was nothing in the children's world, from the most mundane event to the ecstatic limits of sex and death, that did not take its form in the media: "It's as if the film came first for them" (72), the narrator's police accomplice comments, as if this made these children unusual.

Reality, to use Baudrillard's formulation, had been preempted by the "hyperreal."[5] On a perceptual level, of course, reality always involves some degree of representation: you comprehend only what you have encountered in some form before. Unique events inevitably appear as unreal, supernatural if they are powerful enough to cross the threshold of perception at all. Most unique events are mere oddities as far as the conscious mind is concerned, literally insignificant and therefore invisible. Only by virtue of repetition or representation do first appearances emerge in a *nachträglich*, "deferred" construction from an unconscious past: "Ah, now I remember that pause, and it meant he was betraying me." The insidious thing about the hyperreal is that the most important first events,

113

the "originals" from which later events will take their meaning, already have the form of a representation.[6] Baudrillard sees Disneyland, for example, as an event for children against which they later experience cities. Images of smart bombs destroying cities in the Persian Gulf refer inevitably to computer-game imagery and technology. Pleasure seems hardly conceivable unless it follows forms created by advertising and pornography. So Ballard's teen murderers would hardly be unique if for them "film came first."

This intrusion of film and video into postmodern culture has a stabilizing effect on a reality constructed from images: insofar as reality is constituted by the image, it remains representable, and hence understandable, subject to control. Hyperreality implies a total correspondence between the real and the knowable and therefore contains a denial of anything that might exceed or evade representation. As pubescent teenagers, however, the Pangbourne Village children were becoming aware of some unknowable excess through the experience of their own sexualized bodies – alien bodies suddenly bereft of the compact forms and pleasures of childhood. The children looked for the parental guarantee that maturity would compensate them for what has been lost. But for all their parents' wealth and health, the guarantee was empty, the law missing. Jim, the hero of *Empire of the Sun*, says he knew his well-exercised father's strength came from playing tennis and so would fail before the Japanese soldiers, whose strength came from death. The Pangbourne Village parents could not be "supposed to know" – of pleasure, death, reality, and its compensations. The narrator says of the murders, "[F]or such killing to take place at all, the deaths of [the] victims *must* be without any meaning" (81), an observation I take to mean that the adults' *lives* were without meaning, without any reference to the in-you-more-than-you, but limited by the boundaries of the representable, the hyperreal.

The narrator's idea, however, that the children were escaping from their enclosed world into something more real, a realm of the senses, of the imperfect, is not convincing. One child, the youngest, escapes the group, in "a desperate attempt to return to her childhood world" (73), the narrator supposes. The girl, eight years old, had not yet had to face the knowledge of a sexual body with its mark of internal, essential inadequacy, of death. Her parents had probably not yet revealed themselves to be unable to guarantee future pleasures, since she had not yet found her needs to exceed her demands. And so, as the narrator speculates, she might want to return to her childhood and to the supposition that her parents are able to know her to the bone. For the other, postpubescent children, such a direct return is blocked by a knowledge of the adults' impotence, and so the children can return to childhood (and why should they not want to?) only by restaging the past enjoyment through a violation of parental law. The children must now be "far beyond the point where questions of guilt and responsibility have any meaning for them," says the narrator (79), who might just as well say they have returned to a point before the paternal function was implanted, outside the symbolic order formed by the subjugating Law. The "family" formed by the children is without a "ringleader," without a father figure to whom responsibility and guilt are owed for individual actions. In place of the panopticon subjectivities – individualized, separated, penetrated – the children take on the non-individualized identity of the group, a group apparently without an inner life.

The group members achieve "unity," according to the narrator, as a result of their belief in "the rightness of their cause" (80), as if they have substituted a higher law for the one they have denied. The "cause" itself, however, never takes on a positive form but remains denial: they attempt the assassination of "a former British prime minister," evidently Margaret Thatcher, the phallic "Mother of her Nation" (104). Although a failure, the attack has the effect of moving the Pangbourne children back into the media. Unlike terrorists of colonized countries who resort to terror as their only hope of ejecting the dominating power, the West's internal terrorists – the Red Brigade, the Weathermen, the Baader-Meinhof gang – constitute their identities and produce their effect largely with the help of the media. The Pangbourne Village children, then, find a way to reproduce the situation of surveillance in which they came to consciousness. In being observed, they stand again on the stage, objects of a fearfully desiring public gaze.

Reviewers were generally not enthusiastic about *Running Wild*.

James Marcus writes, "The assumptions 'Running Wild' is supposed to challenge, such as the fairy-tale version of family happiness, haven't been widely accepted for decades." Of course, no one is surprised any more to read that the children of privilege kill themselves or others, that they rape their dates, defraud their banks, and ruin lives. The sophisticated population knows very well that the fairy tale is over, but they continue, nevertheless, to see such failures at happiness as confined to mass media reports. Middle-class parents continue to expect, or at least feel they deserve, lives of simple contentment and success for their own progeny and their friends'. On television we see "upheavals, disasters, cataclysmic events of all sorts" but – as Luc Sante commenting on Ballard's writing points out – register them "only as momentary images that are quickly forgotten." Despite the cynical knowledge conveyed by popular media, then, a "fairy-tale version of family happiness" does remain for many of us a model for domestic life. The inability of *Running Wild*'s narrator to produce a convincing analysis of the story he tells may reflect a limitation in Ballard's willingness to understand what he has seen, but the image of damaged children still fascinates and disturbs.[7]

Crash offers a version of the insight Ballard begins to conceal in the later book. Ballard claims *Crash,* often suggestive of Jean Genet, is "the first pornographic novel based on technology" (6). The book is hard to take at times with its insistent return to explicit conjunctions of sexual bodies and automobiles (the mingled smells of semen and engine coolant, for example, are noted frequently). Children are wholly absent from the book, but the erotic fixations have a quality that it is tempting to call childish, or at least adolescent, for their refusal to move beyond the most elemental physical body. If the characters of this novel previously reached a mature level of bodily abstraction, the "genital reduction" that characterizes normative adult sexuality, then something happened to take them back to polymorphous perversity.

The bodies of all the main characters except James Ballard's wife, Catherine (I refer to her husband, who is named after his creator, as "James" to prevent confusion), have been marked by cars, scarred in ways that James insists are completely distinct for each accident, each car, each particular body. Specific knobs, steering wheels, hand brakes, rear-view mirrors, and windows leave their unique inscriptions on knees, faces, and chests. The way a crashing car flips and collapses determines how it will crush and cut a body, juxtapose car parts to body parts, or mix machine fluids with a body's liquid flows. The wounds are horrible and fascinating in their details (Ballard used a richly illustrated book, *Crash Injuries,* by Jacob Kulowski, to give his descriptions a disturbing precision), providing a vision of a body as composed of removable, alterable parts. The body and self do not form an organic whole in this vision. The body as a symbol, as a representation of the self, reveals itself under violence to be the uncanny body, the one that surprises us in hotel mirrors and old photos of our parents in their youth. It is the body of the helpless infant tended by the practical hands of a parent or nurse, the wild body "sunk in motor incapacity and nursling dependence," that Lacan describes flailing before a mirror (1977: 2). That lost body returns through the accident, made present in the changes wrought by the specific technology of a modern industry.

James's initiation into the realm of crash eroticism follows his own head-on collision with the car of Helen Remington and her husband, who is killed in the accident. James and Helen are pinned facing each other, the crushed cars and bleeding body of her husband between them. In this situation they are photographed by Vaughan, a highway angel whose life is devoted to the capture of the crash image or, more specifically, of the way the automobile mediates human relationships (101). Vaughan's images transform the suffering and horror associated with traumatic injury into a scene of erotic enjoyment.

Robert L. Caserio's excellent essay on masochism sees that the power of experiences of immobility lies in their recollection of a "binding moment" of childhood, a primal scene of intense but passive pleasure. In childhood, this pleasure serves the "vital order": what keeps you alive gives you pleasure. Later, it is the repeated joining of the passive position to intense, even painful stimulation that informs suffering with eroticism. Caserio sees in this transformation a creative, restorative power in that one can "be shocked back to where one began, at the verge of the vital order, remembering unambiguous vital functions" (308). In *Crash,* then, "Vaughan has made himself the delegate of Eros to convince highway victims that the roadside slaughter really represents death's binding and defeat by love" (302). In recalling the life forces experienced in childhood, we again experience love as something real, as a force that sustained life in a body unable itself to act, and from that point, Caserio argues, we can reconstruct an adult world of action and mediation.[8] Well, yes, perhaps a reader will glimpse that early paradise and move forward with renewed energy and faith in life, but the characters' restaging of that early pleasure can be fatal. Colin Greenland writing on Ballard notes that "[d]eath . . . offers fixity, an end to change, whereas living merely erodes identity further. Hence our preoccupation with violence and destruction, our demand for more, faster, deadlier cars" (114). As Caserio suggests in a Ulyssean metaphor (300–1), the reader may be tied to the ship's mast as the sirens sing, but the characters all leap into the sea.

The optimism of Caserio's reading of Ballard and science fiction derives from a faith in the human willingness to move repeatedly away from the passive position of childhood pleasure into the symbolic activity of adult life, despite the hollowness attending that displacement of bodily joys. Ballard, on the contrary, however, seems troubled by the deep persistence of the images of perversity, and by the ways the world of technology and consumption appeals to them. James Ballard the character makes television commercials, producing the images that define some of our most common desires and satisfactions, those experienced not through the human creative or productive capacity but in the pseudoactivity of consumption. One of the reasons Vaughan chooses to work with James is that James has access through his work to the glamorous world of film stars: he wants an introduction to Elizabeth Taylor. For Vaughan, as for our culture as a whole, the automobile is unavoidably linked to the deaths of stars. He mentions James Dean and Jayne Mansfield but includes in his obsession with famous car deaths America's most filmic president to that point, John Kennedy, going so far as to drive a Lincoln identical to that in which Kennedy was shot. Vaughan's desire is to extend this set of crash images to include filmic icons

118

not yet fatally injured in cars: Elizabeth Taylor (possibly inspired by the widely reported story that she held Montgomery Clift's bleeding head after a car accident he had leaving her house) and, with astonishing insight for a book published in 1973, Kennedy's filmic successor Ronald Reagan, caught in "a complex rear-end collision" (16).

When Vaughan photographs the victims of accidents, he is concerned with discovering not an adult, social being, but only the subject created in "the interaction between an anonymous individual and his car" (101). The "reinvigoration" of accident victims comes out of Vaughan's ability to give them new bodies, part flesh and part machine, that resemble those prefigured in the "scenes of pain and violence that illuminated the margins of our lives" – the television news, advertisements, and "road-safety propaganda" we see every day (190, 37, 39). James has the impression that his accident is his first "real experience" in years (39), one that brings into accord the images with which he has been suffused and the body he lives in. The sense of rebirth through the crash is reinforced by the recovery process in which nurses "seemed to attend only to my most infantile zones," "guarding my orifices" as the women of his childhood did (33). In this second childhood, he has new orifices in his knees and scalp, through which pus drains. Generally, the adult abandons infantile zones of need and pleasure – those of polymorphous perverse sexuality – but in their new configuration, linked to crash wounds, they constitute the reborn sexual bodies of Vaughan's photographed victims. In a sexual encounter with one particularly badly injured woman, Gabrielle, James finds her body's scars to constitute new sexual organs, more erotic and numerous than conventional sexual zones. By comparison, the body of his wife, her orifices devoid of any trace of snot, ear wax, or feces, is unexciting despite its total availability. If she represents some persistence of a child's pristine body into adulthood – the fantasy of conventional fashion and eroticism – James rejects that body in favor of the new body of violence and technology. Only when he imagines Catherine's destruction is there affection between them.

After his encounter with Gabrielle, James recounts a fantasy concerning his mother:

> I visualized the body of my own mother, at various stages of her
> life, injured in a succession of accidents, fitted with orifices of
> ever greater abstraction and ingenuity, so that my incest with
> her might become more and more cerebral, allowing me at
> last to come to terms with her embraces and postures. (180)

James imagines overcoming the insufficiency of childhood that presents an impossible obstacle to the child's desire for the mother by
creating a new body for the mother. The embrace he can at last
come to terms with is one remolded by machines. The conditions of
the technofantasy overcome the gap between the body and knowledge, reconfiguring them both as a geometry of surfaces. The imagined embrace is more abstract, more cerebral because it proposes a
knowledge that is wholly superficial. Here the parent knows and is
known, without the impediment of a natural body, one full of depths
unmarked by language, one more-than-you.

Lacan sees human sexuality emerging from the conjunction of
two flaws that touch all of us. One is the lack defined within semiotics, the lack in the Other by which the speaking subject is constituted as a split subject: "the subject depends on the signifier and . . .
the signifier is first of all in the field of the Other." It is this split that
opens us to the endless displacements of desire where no object is
ever fully satisfying, where no demand is adequate to the need. The
second flaw lies in the death suffered by any creature that reproduces sexually, as if each of us lacked some part that condemns us
to mortality: "The real lack is what the living being loses, that part of
himself *qua* living being, in reproducing himself through the way of
sex. This lack is real because it relates to something real, namely,
that the living being, by being subject to sex, has fallen under the
blow of individual death" (1978: 205). Ballard seems to be attuned
to this conjunction when he sees that desire for automobiles is not
completed with the presentation of the car body in advertising, no
matter how red the paint and sensuous the line. Satisfaction requires the crash as a permanent background, a death's head more
or less present in the ad. In a typical advertisement, a car powers
through sliding turns above a warning that you, the consumer, not
attempt such a maneuver – lest you die. On a visit to the crash test
site at the Road Research Laboratory, Vaughan says to James:

"The technology of accident simulation at the R.R.L. is remarkably advanced. Using this set-up they could duplicate the Mansfield and Camus crashes – even Kennedy's – indefinitely."

"They're trying to reduce the number of accidents here, not increase it."

"I suppose that's a point of view." (123–4)

As Freud notes in *Civilization and Its Discontents,* many of the ills civilization and technology have managed to cure are themselves the product of preceding advances. Vaughan tends to look not at what the researchers "try" to do but, in much the way Don DeLillo looks at purveyors of insurance, national security, and eternal life in *The Names,* at what they do. What kind of car, after all, asks you to push it through tight, fast turns?

The point is that the crash is already there in the human subject, an effect of the trauma that ruptures the imaginary unity of the infantile world. The consequent emergence of body *parts,* each with symbolic as well as biologic functions (a leg is always more than just a thing to walk on), determines a course of pleasure for the individual subject: loss is attended by promises of recompense. The process of maturation transforms the body parts increasingly into symbolic elements, both excluding the bodily specificity of the part and repressing the nonsymbolized body, banishing it to silent functioning, and malfunctioning. (How disconcerting that hypertension, the "silent killer," part of the unsymbolized body, should intrude on the symbolic body as impotence or blindness, or death.) But this symbolized body can never fulfill the promises of recompense, and maturity means recognizing and accepting this failure. The alternative to this recognition is to disavow loss and to seek a repetition of the crash, a return to that traumatic moment of subjection and enjoyment. James watches at one point as Catherine and Vaughan engage in a "sex act" in the back seat of a car he is driving. Romance, the high form of symbolized body parts, does not appear in the action: "I felt that this act was a ritual devoid of ordinary sexuality, a stylized encounter between two bodies which recapitulated their sense of motion and collision." The ritual in the couple's intercourse has the function of recovering the trauma and the body that went with it. Catherine is described as looking at her breast in Vaughan's hand "as if seeing it for the first time, fascinated by its unique geometry"

(161, 160). Their sex acts recapitulate crashes that recapitulate childhood trauma, that give the subject a new and knowable body, one that can be caressed, cut, photographed, and destroyed.

The pleasure James and the others experience should probably not be construed as a door of liberation, as an access to some Eden of original joys. Such is the interpretation *Running Wild*'s narrator makes of the Pangbourne children's deeds. *Crash* suggests that the catastrophic actions taken by those children might also be read as a desperate reenactment of early pleasures and trauma. In both books, the characters return to the site of the crash because, like Lolita returning to Humbert Humbert's bed every night, they had nowhere else to go. Although the symbolic law has been revealed to be a sham, unable to guarantee the eventual mastery of an unstable world, the subject strives to reinforce the other's desire, to make it real by being the perfect object of desire, the focus of parental surveillance, the victim of trauma. Ballard's characters seem motivated not to find freedom but to repeat situations in which they were fully known, before authority had shown itself incapable of effective action. *Crash* demonstrates less how the perversion originates than the way it has become fully interwoven with the forms of advertising and technology that drive contemporary capitalism. That is, the rational forms of production, marketing, and consumption depend on perpetuating a certain perversion.

Only *The Atrocity Exhibition* provides a more extreme critique of this particular union of capital, love, and technology. The book addresses the general erotic failure of contemporary social relations and, like *Crash*, sees the world of technology and politics conspiring to produce a solution of sorts. For example, one chapter, "Love and Napalm: Export USA," imagines a clinic where "disturbed children[,] terminal cancer patients," middle-income housewives, and others are shown films juxtaposing combat and atrocity footage with shots of various body parts. As a consequence, the patients show improved "levels of overall health and sexual activity" (95). The infamous chapter, "Why I Want to Fuck Ronald Reagan," depicts Reagan purely as a represented body, fragmented and reassembled in polymorphously sexualized arrangements, producing in viewers a level of sexual arousal otherwise impossible for them to achieve. These techniques represent the discovery that "sexual intercourse can no longer be regarded as a personal and isolated activity, but is seen to be a vector in a public complex involving automobile styling, politics and mass communications" (94). That is, the source of sexual desire, which ultimately involves the way we all interact socially, is implicated with the way we do business, a discovery that also suggests why political and military rationales have been unable to explain the "extended duration" of the Vietnam conflict: the conflict and its images had helped the American public establish "a positive psychosexual relation with the external world." It is as if the nation had lost the imaginary ballast that allows human beings to live with the instability of the rational, symbolic world, lost the mother's face that, appearing beside the infant's image in the first mirror of childhood, allows the child to believe in a true, coherent self.[9] The car and camera provide the coherent body we lack, the image of power and independence we aspire to, and advertising, politics, and entertainment insinuate these products into our habits of language and consumption, shaping our capacity for pleasure. In this way the perverse and the political become intertwined.

The origin of Ballard's vision of the modern world may be deduced from the account of his own childhood in *Empire of the Sun*. The novel details the emergence of a particularly American world out of the failures of two traditional forms of social authority: the British form, based on a rigid class structure, and the Japanese, based on a cult of the emperor. Both are profoundly racist. As the boy, Jim (another character named after the author), watches the successive defeats of the two powers, he loses the faith in authority that had anchored his emotional ties to the family and culture and binds himself in its place to the imagery of technology and death that he finds in American war machinery and film.

What is most striking about this novel's depiction of a child's experience of war is that Jim grows to love it.[10] First, when the Japanese come to total dominance, he shows hardly a sign of grief at losing his childhood fantasy of cultural invulnerability and privilege, one shared by most of the powerful white elites of prewar Shanghai. And then, at the end of the war, he cannot bring himself to leave the prison camp to return to his battered parents and England. He is in many ways like the Pangbourne Village children: protected, nurtured, observed, and bombarded constantly with images of his culture. Even in church he would be shown newsreels of his country at war, noble and brave, if not at that moment victorious. And as the evidence of British inferiority to the Japanese emerges, he aligns himself with the Japanese, looking to them for protection and a model of behavior.

Jim's experience differs from the Pangbourne children's, however, in that from early in his life he also sees a realm of grotesqueness in the streets of Shanghai that is clearly beyond anyone's control. The beggar who sits by his front gate does not flinch when his foot is run over, and Jim sees in stark detail the imprint of Firestone tires in the foot. In the streets Jim sees the wounded, deformed, orphaned, and abused, the crush of Chinese at Japanese checkpoints, the careless cruelty of soldiers. He sees the police: "He was fascinated by the gleaming Sam Brownes of these sweating and overweight men, by their alarming genitalia that they freely exposed whenever they wanted to urinate and by the polished holsters that held all their manliness" (15–17). With his acute vision, he sees an excess in his world that is contained only by virtue of the fences, doors, and glass that define the British space. The symbolic world defined by British law, that is, is not absolute but limited, like a game. And like a game, like contract bridge – about which he is writing a book, though he has never played a hand – to succeed is a matter of learning the codes, of submitting not to the apparently transcendent order of the symbolic but to the arbitrary rules of power.

Jim responds, then, to the defeat of the British forces and imprisonment of the foreigners by submitting himself to the apparent power. He attempts, without luck, to "surrender" to the Japanese, and when they ignore him he turns himself over to two Americans, Frank and Basie, opportunistic criminals living off (and on) the margins of Shanghai. What Basie teaches Jim, both on the streets and later in the prison camp, is that survival requires absolute submission to the conditions of power. He reconnects Jim to what Caserio calls the vital order.

This submission does not necessarily imply a conventional desperation, though Jim is not above taking food from someone he sees is about to die. More often it is a matter of abasing himself to someone, of serving. Jim provides the sick Basie with a larger portion of food than he usually manages by helping the servers. Basie says,

"You helped Mrs. Blackburn?"
"I ingratiated myself. I made myself very useful to Mrs. Blackburn."
"That's it. If you can find a way of helping people, you'll live off the interest." (117)

Basie reminds Jim " 'to bow to Sergeant Uchida.' 'I always bow, Basie,' " Jim replies (119), suggesting not self-degradation but pleasure at having discovered this method of surviving. When Basie deserts Jim in favor of two other more promising children, Jim watches "without resentment." "He and Basie had collaborated at the detention center in order to stay alive, but Basie, rightly, had dispensed with Jim as soon as he could leave for the camps" (129). The sense of decent behavior, a morality he would have learned from his parents and his British background, is replaced with a code that is in many ways clearer, one linked to the order of life and death. Jim's understanding of the world here is not governed by the symbolic order, by an authorizing, transcendent law, but by the utterly contingent rule of arbitrary power.

The world into which Jim has moved operates in the realm of detachable parts rather than under the signifier of the phallus. Although the policemen's genitals may be "alarming," manliness is in the holster. More frequently, it is the aircraft that become identified for Jim with power. His childhood bedroom is hung with models of planes, and he learned from early in his life to identify passing aircraft. But it is the conjunction of machine and body that affects him most profoundly. He sits in an old crashed plane's cockpit, hands on the controls "as if this sympathetic action could summon the spirit of the long-dead aviator" (25). This plane sets off a series of "confused emotions" in him, testifying to the place the machine has come to serve in his self-image even before the war. But with the advent of war, this identification becomes solidified as he observes the training and departure of *kamikaze* pilots. The ritual ceremony preceding the lethal flight lent meaning and grace to the act, transforming the man into a part of the weapon. Later Jim will see the captured pilots from a downed B-29 – one of "[t]he huge, stream-lined bombers [that] summed up all the power and grace of America" (236) – and marvels that such a machine could have been "flown by men such as Cohen and Tiptree and Dainty," subordinat-ing the individual man's authority to the machine's, to the spectacle of technology.

Ideas of coherence, integrity, individual worth increasingly come to have little meaning for Jim. All order is determined by the desire of some other who watches, who arbitrarily shuffles parts and people for a greater pleasure. Jim witnesses an attack by American Mustang fighters, looking down on the passing planes from a tower: "His eyes feasted on every rivet in their fuselages, on the gun ports in their wings, on the huge ventral radiators that Jim was sure had been put there for reasons of style alone." "Style" is a matter of parts – com-plex, graceful, and gratuitous, there to feed the eye – and the pilots are hardly more than an additional stylish part. The danger posed by his position of observation is as inconsequential to him as is the pilots' peril. As one Mustang crashes, it "exploded in a curtain of flaming gasoline through which Jim could see the burning figure of the American pilot still strapped to his seat," the pilot becoming a "fragment of the sun." He momentarily grieves for the pilots but welcomes their deaths and his own: "Despite everything, he knew he was nothing" (202, 203, 204). These deaths anticipate the later deaths from the explosion at Hiroshima, which he sees from across the sea and reads as "a premonition of his death, the sight of his small soul joining the larger soul of the dying world" (286). Fulfill-ment comes not in the great globe of life but in submitting to the sun of death.

When writing *Empire of the Sun,* Ballard must have known Nagasi Oshima's *In the Realm of the Senses* (1976), a film in which the characters' perverse relation to the body is connected to the inabil-ity of the emperor of fascist Japan to guarantee the phallic order. A woman who has been dropped by her wealthy lover begins an affair with a married man who refuses to join in the mobilization of the army around him. Both devote themselves to utter sensual exhaus-tion, completely unable to find symbolic gratification in their rela-tionship. Ultimately, she strangles him in erotic extremity, slices off his penis, and walks happily through the streets for days carrying it. For each, the failure of the phallic function (wealthy lover's faithlessness, the increasing disintegration of the empire) reduces the body to a collection of parts. The couple's fatal affair developed from their denial of the law of limited pleasure. And as long as manliness is considered detachable (whether as a penis, gun, car, or plane), the phallus does not exist. Oshima claims the French translation of the title of this film (his favorite of all the translations), *L'empire des Sens,* is a play on the title of Roland Barthes's book *L'empire des Signes,* an exploration of the pleasure of the sign in Japan (Desser 97). Ballard's title *Empire of the Sun* ties sun, *sens,* and *signes* together, linking bodies, the bomb, signs, and sense under an empire that consistently evades the order of the state.

The cheerful Americans turn out to be, even more than the Japanese, the servants of death, in the destruction both of bodies and (ironically for citizens of a country devoted to the idea of the individual) of the distinct, autonomous, meaningful self – the symbolic subject. Jim, late in the novel, is momentarily exhilarated by Basie's suggestion that, because he witnessed the explosion of the bomb, he might "appear in *Life,*" the magazine (347), thereby coming under the combined gaze of "life" and America. But to be in *Life* means in some way to join the world of images that he fed on during his time in the prison camps, not to return to life and become a part of the symbolic world. Jim sees himself as the object of death, and all his actions lead him to fulfill his obligations to death. His minute observations of his own bodily decay – his hollowed eyes, his pus-filled gums – and the deterioration of others (soldiers and prisoners) resemble Vaughan's catalog of bodies marked by crashes. Jim's life during the war is not a deferral of real life (like the reality principle's wise delay of pleasure) but the denial of such deferral, a negation of negation. For it is only as the object of death that he is fully known, perfected in his evident weakness before the world.

Jim's greatest anxiety at the end of the war is that the fighting has really ended. He is convinced that a magazine advertisement he tore out depicts his parents and that they will not recognize him, and in fact they do not. "Poor fellow, you'll never believe the war is over," his rescuer says to him (367). And Jim does not quite believe the news, seeing World War III already under way in postwar Shanghai. Like the Pangbourne children, if what I argue about them is correct, he finds intolerable the thought of leaving the protected compound, the one place where power fully defines the parameters of being. Those who destroyed Pangbourne Village did not escape into freedom and health but re-created home under even more austere conditions, much as the children who found Manson built – in the midst of a life apparently unbounded by any restraint – a totalitarian world. It is the youngest who leads, Manson said when asked if he was the leader, suggesting that children know something about love and pleasure and fear that maturity has enabled most of us to forget. When toward the end of *Running Wild* the children raid a hospital to take back the youngest of the group, it is not unlikely that they come to get their leader, for she is the one who initiated the killings by electrocuting her bathing father.

When Jim departs Shanghai at the end of the book, there is no sense that he is leaving behind the horror of the war. The city itself has in many ways already anticipated what he can expect to find in the West: images of Western technology are projected everywhere; American cars fill the streets; and American soldiers are literally pissing on this corner of the world. *Crash* gives us some idea of what Jim will become, the maker of television commercials, obsessed with the relations among technology and identity and death. Advertising is one development of the claim Don DeLillo makes in *The Names* that this century is on film (200): what is knowable, despite an amazing acquisition of scientific knowledge, belongs increasing to the image. And advertising suggests above all that you really live only in the eye of the camera. Much of the pleasure of what film theory refers to as "classic cinema" derives from the impression that with one more cut the image will be complete, without a gap in knowledge. Advertisements rely on the same idea, for the practice of watching film has lent viewers a habit of submission to the imaginary. In consumption, the image will know you: the car, the camera, the technology will take your body and shape it into a form knowable without gaps.

This surrender is the "death drive" in action – not necessarily the action that will make you dead but the move that submits you to death's liquidation of the phallic authority. The common presumption many of us hold that we can transcend death through the efficacy of the individual soul belongs to the general spiritualization of the body that Western culture accomplished in attempting to deny the utter contingency and helplessness of the individual organism. It has become ever more difficult, however, to maintain this fiction under the conditions of the twentieth century: human paltriness before the the media's constant displays of destruction; the instrumentalization of the body in its cybernetic relation to industrial (and entertainment) technology and its availability to medical techniques; our dependence on sources of knowledge and pleasure that are increasingly beyond any individual's control. Such conditions imply for Ballard the increasing emptiness of the symbolic order and, consequently, the diminishment of its earthly representative, the subject. Whatever may be horrific in this change cannot be found in the cool vision of Ballard's prose. Technology has covered the gap, providing, as *The Atrocity Exhibition* demonstrates, a way of submitting your body to a larger purpose, of deriving pleasure by becoming the object of pleasure. This is, perhaps, the appeal Baudrillard sees in the hyperreal, in becoming a filmic body, death's beloved. And, so, seamlessly are we edited into our culture's desires.

7

FATAL WEST

W. S. BURROUGHS'S PERVERSE DESTINY

Shortly before the suicide of Kurt Cobain, lead singer for the group Nirvana, I heard a cultural commentator say that if you find a kid who listens to Cobain and reads W. S. Burroughs, chances are he also uses heroin. A recent television advertisement for workout shoes featured Burroughs extolling the virtues of technology, his familiar image (black suit and hat, gaunt face) on a micro TV that lies like junk in a wet alley while a high-tech-shod urban youth runs past. In the film *Drugstore Cowboy* (1989), Burroughs appears briefly as the priest-turned-junkie who had introduced the protagonist (Matt Dillon) to drugs and who unrepentantly explains that only squares do not understand that the pleasures of drugs are necessary in a world devoid of delight. Burroughs has become an icon that illuminates the obsessions of American culture where the hopes for ageless bodies and technological fixes are inseparable from the self-destructive fixes of drugs and despair. Whatever Burroughs's conscious critique of the Western world might be, his position as a switchpoint between fixations of perverse longing and healthy aspiration provides a way of examining the currents that underlie the westward path, the American destiny.

Burroughs's writing, with its mockery and disparagement of almost all Western values, looks as if it aims at some subversion of those values, perhaps even at some alternative vision. We might, that is, see him as a political writer aspiring to produce social change, an aspiration like those that animate much post-structuralist writing. But if we do, we are certain to find his critique to be at best secretly conservative, at worst suicidal,[1] which would make him no worse than most ostensible subversives. The failure of subversion seems to be built into most modern political critiques. Baudrillard, for example, shows that Marx's categories of exchange and use value imply his already accepting a capitalist understanding of value (1975: 22–5), freeing Baudrillard himself to pursue a love affair with the very mechanisms of consumption he challenges. Roberto Calasso hears "Marx's secret heart beating" with a pervert's excitement over the possibilities of the "total dominion" of his ideas over the world (227). Kristeva brilliantly demonstrates the ways in which patriarchal forces create a structural cage for women but is unable to articulate a nonparadoxical alternative to the psychosis that comes with any rejection of the symbolic law.[2] Foucault thoroughly explores the institutional forces that constitute the individual within every social context, a critique that has the disadvantage of being unable to suggest methods of resistance beyond the "micro." Butler in *Gender Trouble* attempts to provide a subversive alternative to complement her Foucauldian analysis of gender and produces an ethic of "drag," something unlikely either to worry the repressive forces of gender or to console those most deeply troubled by gender; meanwhile, drag becomes fashion. These examples stand for a theme in critical discourses, both of "subversives" who fail to subvert and of critics who point these failures out.

The reason for failure, however, remains constant throughout the range of texts. Frederick Dolan, arguing Burroughs's entanglement with the culture he attacks, puts Burroughs's argument this way: Burroughs's "central quarrel with Western civilization" centers on the inaccuracy of the "Aristotelian construct":

> "Reality" just *is* synchronous and unpredictable, whereas the declarative sentence moving ahead determinably through time makes it appear as if one event follows another in an orderly manner. Burroughs might attempt to write in ways that undermine the Aristotelian construct, but not without declaring *something*, and finally, as we have seen, not without becoming inveigled in this construct's seductive images of lucidity, order, control, and a plenitude beyond mere writing as fiction. (1991: 549)

Like Poe's perverse universe in *Eureka,* Burroughs's universe does not function according to the rules of logical discourse, of cause and effect. But criticizing Aristotelian reason is easier than escaping it, perhaps because the structure of rational thought always steps in as the judge, converting every voice into its own. Any voice that is not complicit with reason becomes, inevitably, unreasonable. As in capitalism, every challenge to the market (the "green" revolution, for example) becomes a marketing opportunity, the challenger just one more player on the field. The subversive assumes that once the foundations have been exposed to be fictive, have been deconstructed, the structure can be reshaped or replaced to function according to new rules, even rules that ignore the Aristotelian construct. The process of exposure itself, however, seems to transform the subversives, drawing them into the ancient dialectic that ties systematic thinkers to their detractors, that ties "abnormal" sexuality to the "normal," to use Rorty's Freudian metaphor for the relation between Derrida and post-Kantian philosophers (106).

To view Burroughs as part of this failure to subvert the dominance of reason is, at best, to find him to be one more symptom of a general malady, another sad example of Marcuse's one-dimensional man, caught up in "sweeping rationality, which propels efficiency and growth, [that] is itself irrational" (xii). But the readiness to which Burroughs's work opens itself to the charge of failure should be a warning. His contradictions, his reversals of sign and referent (is space conceived of as timeless synchronicity a metaphor for outer space or vice versa?), his general longing for a beyond, and other refusals of logical form betray less a failure within symbolic mastery than an excessive purposeless delight in manipulating the very forms of mastery. Certainly, he feels a deep hatred for what he refers to in his later writings as the "Ugly Spirit." His biographer Barry Miles defines this spirit as "the Ugly American, [driven by] forces of greed and corruption, selfishness and stupidity, of *Homo sapiens* [*sic*] arrogance" (253–4). And though Burroughs derides the manifestations of this spirit, what remains compelling about him is how he represents the sources of control and how he evokes a sublime dimension to life, a real not subject to symbolic strictures.

Rather than reading Burroughs the symptom, then, I want to read Burroughs the sinthome, whose writing stages enjoyment.[3] If Burroughs's iconic doubleness does serve as the switch between health and perversity, it is because the world he represents also stages sublime enjoyment within the contradictions and inverted metaphors of social normalcy. Burroughs fascinates, despite his failures of rational criticism and his at times repellent aesthetics, because he so clearly delights in the violence, sexuality, and bodily luxuriances of disease, beauty, intoxication, and excess that attend the "Ugly Spirit." His subscriptions to *Gun World, American Survival Guide,* and *Soldier of Fortune* (Miles 2–3), for example, flaunt an enjoyment of violent technologies that finds its expression in the various gun-toting figures of his fiction and in his own love of weapons. His misogyny includes an appreciation of homosexual eroticism so boisterous that it leaves no room for women. We might ask with Dolan whether Burroughs's ultimate love of narrative inevitably entangles him in the longings and delusions of the Aristotelian construct, but the political question is whether such conformity with the ugly spirit of the West implies his unwitting accord with that spirit.

When Slavoj Žižek adopts the term "cynical reasoning" to describe much contemporary thought, both popular and professional, he moves a step beyond the stoical position of "suspicion," the resistance of those who would not be duped by delusions of authority.[4] The cynic, by contrast, while not duped, lives as if he were: "I know very well, but all the same . . . ." He stops doubting and resigns himself to living under demands he can never hope to fulfill.[5] He sees the cultural superego's injunctions to be honest, generous, and dutiful as a fool's game, but one he continues to play without being tormented by an awareness of its falsity. As discouraging as it is to deal with such cynics in daily life – it is futile to argue with someone holding this view – an avowed cynicism has the advantage of clarifying the subject's motives: just follow the stupid rules as if they were real, and you get real rewards. Women's magazines have long given a version of such advice to women, telling them that men care only for the appearance of virtue. Marabel Morgan goes so far as to suggest to women that if they merely *tell* their men that they admire them (even though they do not deserve admiration), they can make their husbands love them (64). Cynical reasoning has been easily adopted by popular culture for men as well: "My father always said,

'Buy the best and you'll never be disappointed,' " says the son of wealth in an advertisement for high-end commodities, repeating a claim that is effective despite its obvious fraudulence. He might as well say, "I know very well that cost is no reliable guarantee of quality; nevertheless, when I spend more I feel as if I have the best." Although the consumer is bound to be disappointed (since consumption never removes desire), the advertisement helps transform the commodity into a fetish – that is, into a thing that can provide a perverse enjoyment, despite the lack of satisfaction.

Cynical reason returns the reasoner, surprisingly, to the Cartesian position of stupid obedience: in the absence of certainty, it is better to follow the rules. However, where Descartes gave his obedience to the laws of the kingdom, contemporary ideology dictates that reason guide one to pursue wealth and self-interest. The tremendous appeal of such a position is that merely by following duty, reason, and common sense, one incidentally accrues not only wealth and position but also the special rewards that come to those who adhere most strictly to duty. Those fortunate enough to escape poverty, for example, often find themselves, as a matter of civic duty, in the position of disciplining the poor. Their methods may be doomed to fail (choosing not to feed the children of the poor does not usually make such children into productive members of society), but the experience of inflicting suffering on others can still make the job rewarding. It is difficult to subvert those systems (such as the prison system or the campaigns against imported drugs) that seem to accept as a working principle that they will be ineffective. Burroughs's work seems, rather, to celebrate aspects of modern culture that are often acknowledged (sadly, hostilely, sardonically) to fail. However, he takes as the motive of cultural activity not its intentions to improve life, but its capacity to produce enjoyment. The evil of the Ugly Spirit does not lie in its capacity to produce perverse enjoyment but in its failure to recognize that perversity is what sustains it. Burroughs's achievement is to invert the terms of Western history, imagining a culture developing not out of its impulses toward spirit or wealth but out of the impulse toward enjoyment and a denial of the legitimacy of all authority.

Retrospective Utopia

Cities of the Red Night imagines an alternative history of the Western world beginning one hundred thousand years ago, developing out of the Eurasian plains and reaching into the Americas. This history gives no sense of a utopian past, however, no moment when life was sweet and from which humankind has fallen. The distant past of the Cities of the Red Night was as corrupt as any modern time in its greed, racism, and violence. Nor, on the level of individual history, is childhood a place of innocence: at the conclusion of *Cities,* the narrator recalls a dream:

> I remember a dream of my childhood. I am in a beautiful garden. As I reach out to touch the flowers they wither under my hands. A nightmare feeling of foreboding and desolation comes over me as a great mushroom-shaped cloud darkens the earth. A few may get through the gate in time. Like Spain, I am bound to the past. (332)

An ambiguity in the first line leaves us uncertain whether he dreamed *about* his childhood or *during* his childhood, diminishing the difference between ordinary time and the timeless space of dreams. Within this dream he dreams a second dream, a nightmare of the future. Something happened, we feel, to cast us from the garden into the realm of time and death, into reality. Dreams "[blow] a hole in time" (332), leading us to imagine when we awaken that a timeless, deathless realm must once have existed, before or beyond the trauma, the fall from infant bliss, that marks all historical life. But at no time, even in the dream of a garden, can we touch the flower.

Sublime America, the edenic garden, was from the beginning a denial of every constraint of European history. This founding fantasy imagined America as a land without difference, a fresh green mother's breast of a land, as *The Great Gatsby* describes it, where every child is whole and not riven by fantasies of race, religion, wealth, and class. False from the start, the fantasy has nevertheless found embodiment in numerous icons of American life. The astonishing thing about the people of this land is how readily an image of ourselves as uncorrupted can be evoked in us. Despite the venal

135

motives behind almost all of America's founding adventures that led to the decimation of native populations and the importation of African slaves, we repeatedly affirm our commitment to the propositions of nondifference: that Americans aspire to a color-blind, classless, pluralistic society with many religions, but one god.

Burroughs opens *Cities* with a version of the American story, wherein piracy is neither the nascent form of early capitalism nor, in a perversion of big business, the eventual outcome of wild capital's pillaging every weak spot in the financial field. Rather, it is an originating impulse of liberty. Piracy, rejecting the cover of a national flag, declares the absence of limiting, castrating authority, claiming the right to take all wealth for its own.[6] It expresses, that is, the dream that it is possible to win absolute, stable command of the world's wealth. But wealth under capital is wealth only when it is fluid, endlessly circulated and allowed to function as a signifier. All modern capitalists must, consequently, work with a double consciousness: they recognize that capital, as a signifier, is empty despite its profound effects; at the same time they derive the meaningless enjoyment from money that only a fetish can command, even though the fetishized object is often no more than a fleeting electronic transaction. Piracy, then, embodies the enjoyment of a monetary fetish that legitimate capitalism takes as the incidental consequence of its enterprise, but which is in fact a primary inducement for its labors.

Don C. Seitz, whose story of the pirate Captain Mission Burroughs quotes, recognizes an ambiguity of motivations in idealists: Mission's "career was based upon an initial desire to better adjust the affairs of mankind, which ended as is quite usual in the more liberal adjustment of his own fortunes" (xi). The problem with such a desire to elevate others, as Conrad displayed in *Heart of Darkness*'s fortune-hunting "gang of virtue," is that in remaining ignorant of whence they derive their enjoyment, the "benefactors" of humankind need not question what they attain merely in passing. In saving the less fortunate peoples of the world, the powerful stage master–servant/sadomasochist fantasies that "incidentally" exploit and destroy those who come into contact with them. Burroughs seizes this story of the pirate Mission for its sublime potential, seeing in it an American liberty that might have effectively put an end to the history of industry and capitalism by eliminating need, wealth, and class. But unlike the young Marx, who imagines that the elimination of "exchange value" will produce some authentic existence, Burroughs's imagined community evades the tyranny of authenticity by producing a deliberately and literally staged enjoyment.

Burroughs's characters parody our activities, showing how social, economic, and political motives conceal some more fundamental need. Farnsworth, for example, is the District Health Officer, but he is uninterested in typical ideas of health: he has "very little use for doctors" because they interfere with the function of his office, which is to alleviate suffering, whether it arises from illness or desire:

> The treatment for cholera was simple: each patient was assigned to a straw pallet on arrival and given a gallon of rice water and half a gram of opium. If he was still alive twelve hours later, the dose of opium was repeated. The survival rate was about twenty percent. (4)

The opium cure also works well to relieve Farnsworth of his erections. The conventional medical professionals' fight against the enemy Death all too frequently works counter to their aspirations to relieve suffering. We suffer, quite literally, from life and its ally, desire, both of which project us into a future where we will have evaded death. The wealth we accumulate, like the children we have ("money in the bank," one new parent said of her recent acquisition), stands as a symbolic screen against the Real, an investment in the promise that with time we will increase and not simply waste away. But of course, in the long run, the survival rate is zero percent, a point worth forgetting. Farnsworth's goal is to find what gives pleasure to the body independent of the anxieties of the individual subject about death and failure: he tries to relieve the patient of the fantasy that anyone is capable of any action that will evade death, that consciousness might transcend the body. Opium is, in part at least, sometimes the mechanism, sometimes the metaphor, for this condition – sometimes it is merely a drug to suppress desire, sometimes it represents a state free of time and hence of desire. Through Farnsworth, Burroughs both mocks the medical establishment and suggests an alternative orientation for the practice.

At the heart of all social practices in this book is the stage. When

Farnsworth's opium is gone and he is recovering with his boy Ali, this other alternative to reality appears. In this theatrical performance, he becomes aroused in a sexual "dream tension," during which he smells "a strange smell unlike anything he had ever smelled before, but familiar as smell itself" (11). He awakes to find that he is becoming an alligator whose head is "squeezing the smell out from inside." Burroughs alludes here to the idea that the human brain contains the "reptile brain," a formation that recalls and preserves our reptilian origins. The reptile brain is rich in serotonin, opiate receptors, and dopamine, "a neural sap of vital importance for bringing the total energies of the organism into play" (MacLean 406). For Farnsworth, this brain emerges as a smell connected to some ancient, reptilian sense of the Real that displaces all human consciousness. Farnsworth the alligator, whose body pops, boils, and scalds, ejaculates in an agony of enjoyment. But this apparent metamorphosis and literalization of the lizard brain turns out in the next paragraph to have been merely a theatrical production, the alligator a costume and the jungle a backdrop on stage. So, we are left asking, *is* there actually some access to the lizard brain, and, through it, some immediate access to total bodily enjoyment, or is the passage only a metaphor for a kind of experience Burroughs *hopes* might be possible? We seem to be caught in a familiar Burroughs contradiction, such as we just saw with the opium, where the literal and the metaphoric are interchangeable. However, the enjoyment is real (Farnsworth is fucked by Ali in both situations, though we might ask whether fucking is literal or metaphoric), and Farnsworth's enjoyment connects the two worlds, acting as a switchpoint between reality and the stage. The Real question – both the question I want to pursue and the question of the Real – is what might squeeze the "smell," so intimately strange, out of your own brain and thereby give you access to that ancient sense?

Perhaps the contradiction is more accurately an opposition between delusion and illusion, hallucination and artifice (what we mistake as truth versus what we recognize as constructed) and not between what is real and what is merely staged. The *Real* by definition is not open to perception, not directly available to the mind operating in the symbolic realm. We respond to representations, whether we understand them to be true or fictive. Although enjoyment may once have been evoked by the direct experience of stimulation that presumably floods the infant body, for the speaking person it is mediated by repetition: each subject is constructed by events that must be symbolically restaged as fantasy in order to create enjoyment.[7] Reality, in this context, refers merely to those experiences of the world that we fail to notice as staged. That is, we hallucinate a Real based on the images we perceive, as the suckling child hallucinates "milk" at the sight of a breast. Those who would kick a stone and say "there is reality" betray a desire for a Real as immediate as a rock.

When we seek some experience of sublimity, we look to extremity, whether outward to the grandeur of the natural world or inward to the raw passion of, say, sexuality; but neither the Grand Canyon nor the most intimate sexual acts occur for us unconditioned by previous expectation, images, stories – by theater. If we still derive the sublime thrill, it is because we forget the staging or because, like perverts, we give ourselves over to the fantasy. Too much or too little, as I write above – that is always the problem of pleasure. The Aristotelian construct may stand like a firewall between the subject and enjoyment, but the perverse subject can use it as a backdrop against which to stage a fantasy.

Virus and Vampire

Viruses and vampires exert a fascination in contemporary imagination for similar but opposing reasons. Viruses, intruding invisibly on the level of DNA, remind us as their progeny emerge within our own cells that our bodies are not our own.[8] These secret guests arouse in us an abjection that holds the consumer's attention through popular magazines, books, television, and film, as demonstrated by the wealth of stories about ebola, a virus exotic in America, that liquefies the internal organs so that they pour out of any orifice. Viruses illuminate the silent interior of the body, a flesh that is close, vital, and familiarly strange as only our mothers' has been to us. The vampire's appeal, however, is sublime: flesh that refutes time and mortality, that limits its knowledge of the body's interior to blood sucked from another as a baby sucks the breast, preserving beauty, longing, and passion.

139

At the heart of our interest in both viruses and vampires, however, is the recognition that "life" does not favor the living organic body but the "undead" core of memory. Bodies live to reproduce DNA, which is itself non-organic and immortal and which would happily have us bite off the heads of our mates during intercourse if that would favor successful reproduction. Viruses are simple replicating nucleic acids, DNA packages that appropriate the liquid interior of cells for their own ends. In the virus we see the hopeless insufficiency of our bodily selves, our submission to an inhuman process even when that process is our own DNA's survival. The vampire, however, although it also appropriates our liquid interior, represents a fantasy through which we can identify with the inorganic force of replication. The appeal and the horror of both are related to their disregard for the rational subject and its autonomy: something in you exceeds the limits of you, something you do not identify with as *you* and which follows a path that is not yours. Burroughs's well-established hatred of "control" – the insidious compulsions of sex and drugs as they are tied to corporate interests – finds its expression in the ways the viral/vampiric human can be appropriated by social forces and turned to other ends.

Burroughs does not suggest, however, that we might evade such social subjection by "curing" the virus: as one character suggests, " 'any attempts to contain Virus B-23 will turn out to be ineffectual because we carry this virus with us. . . . Because it is the *human virus*' " (25). The virus's symptoms (such as uncontrollable sexual desire) are those of "love": the human virus ("known as 'the other half' ") constitutes our knowledge of our inadequacy, our mortality. We are double, and yet that part of ourselves with which we identify will vanish while the undead within us continues.[9] Conventionally, we deny this knowledge when we speak of the soul as the immortal part of each person. The idea of the soul inverts the relation between body and mind, claiming that the physical vanishes while the soul, a representation of consciousness as unembodied spirit, lives on, untouched by time. In fact, the opposite is more likely true, since consciousness is usually the first thing to go. The account of the Cities of the Red Night retells the story of the immortal soul, stripping it of its sublime dimension and linking it to a history of social power, a practice by which the strong reproduce their kind at the expense of the weak.

The Cities' most distinctive practice involves their refusal of sexual reproduction, of bodies and mortality. The chapter entitled "Cities of the Red Night" lays out the system of "transmigration" of spirit, displaying the interdependence of two classes, Transmigrants and Receptacles:

> To show the system in operation: Here is an old Transmigrant on his deathbed. He has selected his future Receptacle parents, who are summoned to the death chamber. The parents then copulate, achieving orgasm just as the old Transmigrant dies so that his spirit enters the womb to be reborn. (154)

The denial of death by elite Transmigrants – those who consider the perpetuation of their spirits more valuable than that of their mere bodies – leads them to appropriate not just the sexuality of others but the orgasm itself, the males' at least, for the purpose of cultural reproduction. This system leads inevitably to "mutters of revolt" by the women, who see most directly how their enjoyment has been channeled for social designs: women produce children for the pleasure of others (155). In addition, the practice produces "a basic conflict of interest between host child and Transmigrant" (158) since the point of being born is to serve for a few years as the vessel for another's spirit, at the end of which the host submits his body to orgasmic death, again all in the interest of maintaining the Cities' power structure. The solution to this conflict is to "reduce the Receptacle class to a condition of virtual idiocy": that is, children must find their body's enjoyment only through service to the City. One of the inadvertent outcomes of this practice is that the Council of the Cities "produced . . . races of ravening vampire idiots" (157).

The denial of mortal limitation, as the story represents it, leads the elite to abuse power and turn away from the thought that derives from recognizing death. As sublime as the concept of soul may be, it is easily adapted to a system that perpetuates those who are spiritually deserving, which the powerful always consider themselves to be. Perhaps history could have developed otherwise. *Cities* locates the "basic error of the Transmigrants" in their desire to bypass the "basic trauma" of conception. Conception, after all, requires the most fundamental loss of integrity in the splitting of DNA and a rejoining of sexually halved chromosomes. The particular result of conception is fundamentally uncontrollable, subject to the chaotic slippage of dynamic systems and tending toward a purposeless complexity. Evolution – viable genetic mutation – proceeds for the good of neither the individual parent nor the species but, like an artist of serendipity, will try anything, even though a stray "success" (it lives!) may destroy everything that came before.

The Transmigrants, then, are justified in fearing conception, as should all cultures that exalt stability over change. The ultimate collapse of the Cities during the radioactive period of the Red Night ("a time of great disorder and chaos") resulted from the introduction of mutation – change, complexity, and diversity – into a culture devoted to exact replication. Conception, that is, is at odds with "spirit," the reputed essence of an individual ego. Something else within you, something in-you-more-than-you, works silently toward a future. Call it DNA, the Drives, the Human Virus: components of the body work without regard for the spirit, soul, or individual body. But they are represented through the individual body as horrible and thrilling enjoyment, depicted in this story as orgasm; and enjoyment, unless it is channeled by culture, undermines all practices that depend on control – and what social practices do not?

Burroughs suggests that one way of distinguishing cultures is by the way they control enjoyment. In a series of statements about the relationship between what is true and what is permitted, the following claim is associated with America: "Everything is true and everything is permitted" (158). The genius of America is to pretend that despite the absence of limits, the structure of symbolic meaning remains intact, able to guarantee truth: enjoyment is not only possible and good, it is obligatory. The pretense is what enables large parts of American culture to channel enjoyment so effectively – through advertising, entrepreneurial business (as in evangelical meetings of Mary Kay Cosmetics distributors), patriotism, and ecstatic religions – without the disillusionment that characterizes most other, older cultures. Everything is true!

Such is the interpretation the most American of the Cities of the Red Night gave the "last words of Hassan i Sabbah, Old Man of the Mountain": "Nothing is true. Everything is permitted" (158). The words are obscure, at best. It would take a culture such as that which introduced the zero into Western mathematics to recognize both that *nothing* is true (more true than *something*) and that everything is permitted ("whatever is, is," as Parmenides put it).[10] Each of the Cities gives its own interpretation of the sentences,[11] inserting its own fantasy into the tautological emptiness of the juxtaposed claims. In the statement "Everything is true," Burroughs suggests that in a contemplation of Nothing, the American fantasy is to see a hint of the sublime, of a totality beyond expression.

Many of the sequences in *Cities* parody conventional attempts to reach beyond the linguistic medium. In sexuality, for example, we imagine that we move through ecstasy toward freedom: in sex, we seem to transgress the human realm of law, convention, and restraint and to approach a reality that is fully physical, bodily. For Burroughs, however, no activity is more clearly bound to the stage. We see this staging in the passages involving Port Roger, the pirate's home base. The port is itself a set that Burroughs compares to Prospero's enchanted island, and the pirate's main weapon for establishing an alternative society is magic – that is, staged illusion: "It is our policy to encourage the practice of magic and to introduce alternative religious beliefs to break the Christian monopoly" (105). Christianity, in this vision, works by the same rules as other magical productions, so one has only to perform the part of a devout believer to undermine Christianity's status as truth: a ceremony is above all a performance, transcendence an effect.

Recognizing the family to be one of the fundamental institutions of Christian control, the pirates exploit the performance aspect of family: they enlist members of their community to become "families to operate as intelligence agents in areas controlled by the enemy" (106). For families to operate, they must have children. To this end, the pirates gather all the young men and women for a mass dance and insemination:

> Juanito announces: "Rabbit men and rabbit women, prepare to meet your makers." He leads the way into a locker room

opening off the east wall. The boys strip off their clothes, giggling and comparing erections, and they dance out into the courtyard in a naked snake-line. The women are also naked now. What follows is not an unconstrained orgy but rather a series of theatrical performances. (108)

The more orgiastic and unconstrained sex appears to be, the more it requires the careful preparation and control of the governors. What Burroughs displays is not a more authentic vision of family and sexuality than exists in conventional life, of course, but a parody that reveals how readily sexuality can be turned to the service of a state, the pirates' state in this case. As Don DeLillo reveals in his account of the mass wedding staged by the Reverend Sun Myung Moon in Yankee Stadium, the most sublime, mystical events can derive their power from showmanship.

Unlike Marxist critics of such cultural issues, Burroughs is less interested in how institutional power shapes its subjects by instilling an ideology than in how the staging of enjoyment serves as a means of social control. Even when Burroughs seems most intent on imagining a way to escape the forces of social control, for example, he tells us more about how those forces work than about possibilities for actual liberation. Dink Rivers, one pirate character, demonstrates the utility of staging enjoyment when he explains the way a "magical brotherhood" achieves total bodily control, the ultimate aim of which is to escape all unconscious symbolic determinants:

> "At the age of fourteen, when I began to have dreams that culminated in ejaculation, I decided to learn control of the sexual energy. If I could achieve orgasm at will in the waking state, I could do the same in dreams and control my dreams instead of being controlled by them." (127)

The technique requires him deliberately to relive a wet dream. "'I ran through a sex dream like reciting my ABCs'" (128). His model for "reliving" is the recitation of his ABCs, by which he exploits a symbolic form to get at its presymbolic ground[12]:

> "I used the same method of projecting myself into a time when my mind seemed empty of words . . . [producing] a vertiginous

144

sensation of being sucked into a vast empty space where words do not exist." (128)

In projecting himself backward to that originating moment, he finds that his mind *seems* empty of words. However, that moment is always a *nachträglich* construction, an illusion of wordlessness constructed out of the limitations we experience within language, an illusion of freedom made from the constraints of subjectivity. The "dying feeling" Dink describes is a momentary lapse of subjectivity, a feeling many long for (and pursue in drugs, alcohol, sex, and religion) and one they misconstrue as death.

Dink's control of orgasm is based on Zen traditions of bodily control and tantric sexuality, practices that, despite the regular supply of sex manuals they inspire, remain exotic for Americans. However, American institutions employ recitations little more complex than the ABCs to bring crowds of people to this extremity of deathly, linguistic oblivion, a circumstance DeLillo dwells on in *The Names*. We see such practices in religion and political assembly, in action on the stock exchange floor, and in other events that are socially useful yet inspire a sublime thrill. But when someone stages such enjoyment for himself, we know him to be perverse rather than admirable.

The difference between the pervert and a futures trader sweating and screaming like any Pentecostal is that the pervert *knows* what he wants while the other comes to it inadvertently in the course of his duties. This power of the word to produce ecstasy finds expression in one of Burroughs's dream images: the dreamer sees a body spattered with "a shower of red sparks" that create "burning erogenous zones that twist and writhe into diseased lips whispering the sweet rotten fever words" (277). In Burroughs's imagination, every part of the body can be eroticized by a tongue of flame, but the forms those parts take are likely to be abject. The vampire's kiss may look like love, but its aim is blood. The vampire, the ad man, and the evangelical fundraiser on television will, if they know their jobs as well as Poe's diddler, drain you and leave you wanting to give more. The most reasonable language carries something ancient within it that can give speech an elemental power.

The One God Universe Con

Dolan points out that Burroughs's valuing of space over time, of an escape from time's compulsion, allies him with a romantic strain, a gnosticism in American thought, as Bloom refers to it.[13] His writing implies a desire to evade the constraints of the individual psyche in favor of something larger and more persistent. We see this impulse played out repeatedly: in the preference Burroughs shows for polytheism over the "OGU," the soul-mastering, thermodynamically fading One God Universe (1987: 113); in his disregard for chronology in *Cities,* which allows the same character to appear anywhere within a 300-year period; in his preference for the cut-in in the investigative work of Clem Snide and in his own writing.[14] In a world so insistently governed by the ideals of progress and accumulation that make a capitalist economy possible, such a dream of timelessness inevitably looks like nostalgia. The desire that drives capitalism depends on notions of a need that can be remedied through production and consumption. The resulting velocity of cultural change produces a "complexity" that we come to depend on for survival, and it cannot be undone. But as Burroughs implies, the past persists, encrypted in complexity, and we would be as foolish to ignore it as we would be to attempt to return to it. Within the progress of civilization and the entropic waste of time lie generative, productive patterns that endure and return.

The model of memory that Freud presented in *Civilization and Its Discontents* places memory outside of time, with the implication that past events are never recovered as separable, independently standing moments but are imbricated in foundational patterns of mind. Philip Kuberski's *Persistence of Memory* draws out the correspondences between Freud's layered cities, our timeless unconscious, and the compacted history of life contained in DNA. We achieve our sense of linear movement through time only by denying the evidence that time is less an arrow than a tangled vine. The temporal development of dynamic systems tends to produce not unique forms but spatially transformed replications of the same. One implication of this view of temporal development is that the production of constantly varying elements leads not to wholly original forms but to the same on a different scale.

Although he is working from a different model, Burroughs seems to take the implication literally: he disregards the idea that character is located in a unique and perishable individual, seeing instead that a character can arise repeatedly from given circumstances. Consequently, he "reincarnates" characters from century to century as easily as he carries his characters from book to book. Vampires create the vampire anew over generations; viruses transform diverse organisms into replications of the same disease; and language, for all its subtlety, transforms lumps of human infancy into subjects as alike as a patch of cats. But while the human subject develops out of a specific linguistic culture, the body is nearly eternal and governed even more strongly by ancient patterns. More than 90 percent of all human DNA is identical. If an individual wished to evade the determinations of cultural power, the trick would be to get at that common flesh that links one to the eternal, to something older than this culture.

In Burroughs, one of those tricks, "sex magic," employs a ritual that divorces sex from its functioning within a social practice and provokes something ancient and non-individualized in the body. Preparing for a performance, one character says, "According to psychic dogma, sex itself is incidental and should be subordinated to the intent of the ritual. But I don't believe in rules. What happens, happens" (1981: 76). And what happens is that "pictures and tapes swirl in my brain" as the many gods appear and The Smell (that primordial essence of the lizard brain I mention above) surrounds the performers (77). Sex magic, it seems, provides access to knowledge and power that does not derive from the individual subject's reasoning intelligence or talents. Clearly, most sex is not magic: the magic requires one to turn over evolution's gift of orgasm to the proper staging. The ritual requires the performer to submit to the pleasure of some Other, forgoing his or her own desires in order to approach the ancient, the Real: earth knowledge. But in Burroughs's world, the ritual is important because there is no alternative source of power and knowledge.

In earlier chapters, I have considered what happens when authority fails, and the father, the state, the phallus, or whatever we would call the figure that holds the symbolic world in place is unable to promise enjoyment at the end of a long life of repression and self-denial. Burroughs addresses a world in which all authority has revealed itself to be a con game, where the Aristotelian construct that Dolan refers to has shown its hand. But since you cannot, apparently, ignore or directly challenge the construct, you beat a con with another con. Burroughs's image of one con that can resist is the NO:

> natural outlaws dedicated to breaking the so-called natural laws of the universe foisted upon us by physicists, chemists, mathematicians, biologists and, above all, the monumental fraud of cause and effect, to be replaced by the more pregnant concept of synchronicity. (1987: 30)

Burroughs connects this NO figure in *The Western Lands* to Poe's diddler (31), the grinning figure who takes his pleasure in providing people with the illusion they desire, and who also takes their money. (See "Re-Poe Man," Chapter 2 in this volume.) This con, like others, depends on the illusion that the diddler can deny limits, deny death. That is, the NO's breaking of natural laws mimics the perverse wish implicit in phallic authority – enjoyment will one day be yours – except that he offers the reward now. The NO challenges two biologic laws: against crossbreeding between unrelated species and against evolutionary reversibility. Both say that each individual's pleasure is limited, that each of us is on a narrow track to personal extinction, a mere tool of evolution. And what is the God of the "OGU," the One God Universe, but a promise that despite the inevitability of thermodynamic decline, despite "sickness, famine, war, old age and Death" (1213), you, personally, are immortal. The NO plays the same con, offering the perverse where the sad mortal longs for the sublime.

The contradictions that mark Burroughs's writings as argument are demonstrated nowhere more clearly than in the doubling that occurs between the outlaws he values and the figures he most despises. For example, Burroughs seems to promise that those with courage and dedication might travel to the Western Lands, a trip "beyond Death, beyond the basic God standard of fear and danger" where one gains access to "Immortality" (124). But every guide to the lands, from those of the Egyptians and Tibetans to the Messiah, is simply working a con on those desiring eternal life:

148

Messiahs on every street corner transfix one with a confront
stare:
   "Your life is a ruin."
   "We have the only road to personal immortality." (126)

If you turn over your life, they will provide you with a way of
evading the biologic imperative of death. It is an unlikely story, but
Burroughs does not provide the true pilgrim with an alternative, a
true road. These obvious cons, however, mimic the offers made by
legitimate religions, advertisers, and the other operators that inhabit our real western lands. Burroughs cannot subvert these assur-
ances of future happiness except by pointing out the way rational
culture has *always been perverted,* has always linked reason to an
unreasonable expectation of enjoyment.

We should not be surprised that Burroughs's attention to divine
vampires has coincided with an explosion of popular interest in this
figure, ranging from Anne Rice's soft-porn romances to Hollywood's
productions. One big-budget film, for example, seems to have been
written by a Burroughs fan. *Stargate* explicitly links the Egyptian
origins of monotheism to an intergalactic, time-traveling vampire
who passes himself off as the One God to ensure a steady supply of
victims. What is particularly surprising is that the utterly blasphe-
mous nature of this film went unnoticed: its claim that the bloody
God of Judeo-Christian religions is merely a cover story for the
vampire has, apparently, already been too fully accepted by popular
culture to be worth mentioning. Burroughs, the pop icon, may be
so readily accepted by youth because he comes out of the perverse
yet familiar heart of the West.

The sustaining delusion in the Western world is what Burroughs
calls the "fixed image," which he associates with the "basic mortality
error" (158). This fixed image – God, Truth, the Phallus, or any
other figure that says, like Parmenides, whatever is, is; whatever is
not, is not – is behind the monotheistic promise of the individual
soul's survival. It suggests permanence – even beyond death – when
there is always change. The error allows us easily to link sexuality to
reproduction: our longings for immortality are so strong that we
have no trouble taking sexual appetite to imply a drive to make
copies of ourselves, as if the vast liquidity of the bodily Real mani-

fested an unchanging purpose. The romance of the fixed image is allied to perverse fixations, but it provides the perverse the guise of an economic, social, and spiritual good. Economically, this romance implies the reproduction of the means of production by means of an infinitely replicating ideology; biologically, the immortal extension of oneself through children; spiritually, the immortality of one's double, the soul. The fantasy of the fixed image denies temporality – at least when time is conceived of as the wasting stream of entropic decay – by positing a self not subject to degeneration. Burroughs's undermining of this "mortality error" also helps explain his attack on "sex" ("Sex is the basis of fear, how we got caught in the first place and reduced to the almost hopeless human condition" [201]), as well as his rejection of the female (the god Ka "is the only defender against the female goddesses of sexual destruction and orgasm death" [103]). These attacks represent his refusal of the tendencies to use sex and women as defenses against human mortality. The "human covenant" (180) that keeps humans bound to the fixed image is a version of the oedipal contract that we make with the One God: limit your desire, and you will be immortal.

The fixed image, of course, is incompatible with the reality of reproduction. After all, in reproduction the image is subject to chaotic fluctuation as genes err, language slips, and time and accident happen. The "biologic revolution" Burroughs imagines would cause "unimaginable chaos, horror, joy and terror, unknown fears and ecstasies, wild vertigos of extreme experience, immeasurable gain and loss, hideous dead ends" (112). Sounding like Nietzsche here, Burroughs mixes perspectives, giving us both the danger such a step would pose to the rational world and the ecstasy it could bring. But the chaos he describes is no longer just a paradoxical problem leading to a cultural impasse; rather, it has emerged as a solution within contemporary chaos theory. The apparently romantic step that Burroughs proposes – "from word into silence. From Time into Space" (115) – gestures toward the sublime ("awakened pilgrims catch hungry flashes of vast areas beyond Death to be created and discovered and charted"). But it also suggests that one might let go of the commitment the West holds to linear trajectories of meaning and motion that culminate in the presence of Voice and Truth. Burroughs writes, "imagine you are dead and see your whole

150

life spread out in a spatial panorama, a vast maze of rooms, streets, landscapes, not sequential but arranged in shifting associational patterns" (138). That is, to imagine your "self" dead means to imagine that the parts of your life are not fixed by sequence, but by shifting patterns of connection: "This happens in dreams of course." Dreams tell us something about a condition of our lives that we call being dead or, rather, beyond dead. By comparison with the linear path of life, this image of death is vividly dynamic. Chaos does not refute the necessity of temporality – dynamic change, whether in physical systems or in dreams, is irreversible – but the fixed intention, the target of time's arrow, vanishes. In "chaos," one loses the delusion of individual purpose, direction, control, which was why the One God put an end to it. The image that chaos and the theory of complexity substitute for control is the dynamic order of the developing image, of the fractal patterns generated by nonlinear equations, where scale replaces time as complex development replaces purposeful growth.

Burroughs's curious preoccupation with the figure of Hassan i Sabbah, Imam of the Assassins, corresponds to his disregard for the significance of the individual subject: not only do his effective assassins kill individual political figures without remorse, but they willingly accept their own deaths. If one's enjoyment is in submission, the persistence of a personal soul or image might be less important than it would be to one committed to individuality. Burroughs quotes Hassan i Sabbah:

> "It is fleeting: if you see something beautiful, don't cling to it; if you see something horrible, don't shrink from it, counsels the Tantric sage. However obtained, the glimpses are rare, so how do we live through the dreary years of deadwood, lumbering our aging flesh from here to there? By knowing that you are *my agent,* not the doorman, gardener, shopkeeper, carpenter, pharmacist, doctor you seem to be." . . . So acting out a banal role becomes an exquisite pleasure. (200)

In his identification with the figure of HIS, as he calls him, Burroughs finds a way of placing himself outside of any political or economic order, precisely because the "concept of salvation through assassination" (202) is ultimately a parody of the social forces he detests, made perverse in his case by its deliberate exploitation of the enjoyment one can derive from being the agent of another.

The idea of the Western Lands reaches back to Egypt and into a version of America, to the land of the dead and beyond death, to the dream of Hassan i Sabbah and that of Captain Mission. There is a fatality in Burroughs's vision of history, and consequently his critique never develops a clearly external position, never offers an alternative that does not fall into the same history he mocks. This mockery, this con, this clowning queer vision shows that the American sublime shares its soul with the perverse. But I hesitate to call this writing subversive. Burroughs comments on the Arab world's having led civilization to become what it is, in part, by "introducing such essential factors as distillation for drunkenness, and the zero for business. What would Burroughs and IBM do without it?" (198). Alcohol, pathway to both the sublime and the abject. The zero that enables us to signify the Nothing, the Real that defines us, and that made double-entry bookkeeping possible; the zero that made the Burroughs Adding Machine Company and IBM, but that also made W. S. Burroughs. The inseparability of the two aspects of transcendence – below and beyond – suggests less subversion than contamination. Burroughs with his black suit and his dead, knowing eyes brings both the vampire's glamorous seduction and the virus's infection to our vision of American culture, adding a touch of abject enjoyment to the icons of the West.

Can anyone doubt that Burroughs did the athletic-shoe commercial for any reason other than money? But given that motive, could anyone who has read Burroughs, who has seen Burroughs in *Drugstore Cowboy*, who even got a good look at the pale face and hooded eyes on the tiny TV screen, watch the commercial without deriving a peculiar enjoyment inappropriate to simple consumption? What kinds of enjoyment does Burroughs add to the enactment of a ritual purchase that improves the body and drives the economy?

8

CONCLUSION

AGENCY IN THE PERVERSE

In the Macedonian film *Before the Rain,* a spray-painted image of a broken circle appears on a London wall. It is a figure that comes increasingly to the fore throughout the film, ultimately shaping its structure. The film concerns conflicts between peoples that are both personal and deeply historical at a moment when the world waits to see if the Bosnian wars will spill in full force into the neighboring lands, then into the rest of Europe and beyond. In a disconcerting but ultimately dazzling series of scenes, the chronological sequence of events begins to fold, repeating moments in ways that invert before and after, cause and effect. Certain traumatic events seem not to be left in the past but return to provoke later events and reignite earlier passions. Where initially these events had seemed to explain the course of local history and given the characters meaning in their lives, they later come back to confuse every cause. When precisely does a martyr die? What does the death mean? How does change occur? Do we always live before the rain, always awaiting relief?

Each of the three episodes that make up the film depicts a horrific killing. In the first, a girl is killed by outraged relatives for having gone with a boy from the other side. Next, a bystander is killed in a London restaurant during a violent dispute between Balkan antagonists living in Britain. The two events seem to demonstrate the dogged stupidity of violence that produces brutal repetition when the cause no longer seems relevant. More problematic, however, is the killing of a photographer in the third episode. He has returned from London to his native Macedonia in middle age at the height of his fame as a photojournalist, a wandering son made good. After having traveled and worked amidst the violent of the world, however, he has lost the Macedonian's native sense of the small differences that justify the current local enmity between Albanian Muslims and Macedonian Christians: he does not know instinctively whom to hate. He attempts to reconcile his former friends, now one another's enemies, but late in the film, after his large-minded good will has proved ineffectual, he intervenes in the cycle of violence. He places himself between a Muslim girl and the Christian men who would kill her, and in doing so he is killed by his own cousins. Although this event occurs near the end of the film, we soon learn that his funeral also opened the film, where his killing seemed to be part of the motivating violence throughout the story. This man – both professionally disillusioned and personally resigned – acts, but he acts without any way of governing or being able to foresee the consequences of his actions.

In discussions of the film with friends, I found a pessimism about the possibility that this circle of violence, broken or not, might end. When every position that any man or woman occupies seems to be defined by a relation to violence, every action, no matter how well intentioned, is drawn into the dynamic of historical events. The martyr for peace is all too easily appropriated as a martyr for nationalist rage. There is, one person told me, no place to insert oneself into the circle to make a change, a claim the film seems to support. This claim grows out of the wish, I believe, that someone might act to achieve a desired end: that individual agency would produce a desired consequence, that human spirit could become action. Well, what modern person does not work assuming, or hoping, this agency is possible? What successful capitalist would not tell you that his business emerged from his design, that Henry Ford had an idea? Activists must have dreams to direct them. And when the film ends before the rain (despite the intervening downpour), it seems to confirm, by its negative example, the hopelessness of a world deprived of effective agency, where good intentions contribute only to endless conflict. The question I ask is how are we to make sense of the motives for action in the face of such repetition?

Pathological Production

In the first of the *Three Essays on the Theory of Sexuality,* Freud distinguishes between a pathological perversion and the perversions of everyday life. A perversion is, simply, any of those "sexual activities which either (*a*) extend, in an anatomical sense, beyond the regions of the body that are designed for sexual union, or (*b*) linger over the intermediate relations to the sexual object which should normally be traversed rapidly on the path towards the final sexual aim" (150). The "pathological character in a perversion is found to lie not in the *content* of the new sexual aim but in its relation to the normal" (161). The perverse for Freud, like the "pathological" for Kant, lies in actions pursued without regard to a productive outcome, to duty, though such perversities do not become "pathological" to Freud so long as actual copulation results (the "normal" outcome). Normal sexuality, then, is constituted by the submission of normal perversity to the law of good works, reproduction. The problem with this formulation, as Freud well knows, is that reproductive sex is the last link to be generated in sexuality, the recruitment of enjoyment by an agentless development we call evolution, for the dissemination of the species. Without the perverse, nothing happens, at least as far as the world of human sexuality is concerned.

The human subject is not so bereft of good intentions as is brute sexuality, but it is only slightly more capable of self-evolution than the species. We are as a whole at least as destructive of our world as we are productive, producing a positive excess only of ourselves. We are wracked by desires for things we do not – in fact cannot – have but that nevertheless drive us out of bed each day. We don't know where we are going, and mostly we go in a circle – but one that does not close. The dynamic of natural systems introduces chaotic change and complexity, variations that disrupt impulses toward closure. The question that arises, then, is whether significant change (change that is not merely random) is possible without the assistance of subjective agency. The optimistic claim of capitalism that wealth arises from individuals in pursuit of their private ends would reflect a stupendous piece of good luck in the evolutionary path if in fact ends were private in any sense except that some money is in my pocket. I argue throughout this book that private ends are profoundly perverse, and only the appropriation of those very ends by cultural forces can produce culture. And insofar as those cultural forces disguise our perverse enjoyments in the garb of nationalism, racial or economic privilege, ethnic purity, or theocratic governance, the pessimism of my friends is justified.

Directed change succeeds only by eliminating alternatives, either before or after the fact, that do not correspond to the plan. To anticipate, to calculate, and thereby to create a future is the distinctive trait of humans, the bringing into being of things that once had existence only in the word. But there is a profoundly conservative element to this model since all futures are recursively linked to a past, to an attempt to reproduce what is already known. When Freud discusses those things that give us the most profound pleasure, and which we consequently seek most eagerly to repeat, he notes that they are from their first appearance a repetition, linked to a process of reality testing that characterizes our capacity for judgment (1905: 50–1). It is as if we ultimately delight in nothing but the Real, the touch that brought us into being. However, the very process that turns the Real into the enjoyable breaks our connection to the Real. In a curiously enigmatic section, Freud discusses what is necessary for the "sexual aim" to come about:

> it consists in replacing the projected sensation of stimulation in the erotogenic zone by an external stimulus which removes that sensation by producing a feeling of satisfaction. . . . [I]n order to remove one stimulus, it seems necessary to adduce a second one at the same spot. (50–1)

Most of what it means to be human seems to be implied in this replacement of our relation to real needs with a sexualized, symbolic one. The meaningful overwrites the Real, which implies that all sexuality, because it derives from a swerve away from some "original" moment, is secondary, a part of culture.

The consequence of this swerve is that we become human, afflicted with sexuality, a thirst for knowledge, a sense of homelessness in the world. For better or worse, we must create the reality we live in upon these transformed sites of "stimulus." The pervert is merely one who lingers closest to some initial site of transformation, linked by historical accident to a specific past. Normal life, however, erases even that past, overwriting it with the local lessons of culture, channeling desire into meaningful, recognizable forms. This channeling, after all, is what makes the reproduction of culture happen, private aims serving cultural goals; however, channels do not encourage change. Change requires not only will, but accident, the intrusion of the haphazard event, the uncontrolled piece of history with its destructive, as well as constructive, potential. As evolution depends on the errors that enter into the process of DNA replication – errors that are usually meaningless, occasionally fatal – some error in the replication of human culture prevents the circle from closing.[1]

Following great calamities that our fellows occasionally inflict upon us – the assassinations of presidents, the downing of airplanes packed with people, the bombing of an abortion clinic or a federal building – nearly every public voice looks for some active, deliberate agency that could have planned and executed such a deed. And in nearly every case, the proximate cause turns out to be something we call accident or madness or both. This is not the case only in America with its long history of carelessness and passions, but in the bloodfests that have dramatically marked this century, this decade. With the excuse of the Cold War gone, Americans watch with excitement and anxiety as the United States continues to project itself into foreign affairs, such as the fragments of Yugoslavia, not only without a clear purpose but without even the possibility of one. Don DeLillo's *Libra* explores the limitations of agency in the case of Kennedy's assassination, following, rather, the complex web of fantasies that create unintended and unforeseeable events. No conspiracy, the book suggests, could have formulated and executed the complexity that flowered from the multitude of "private" aims. Only in retrospect do the pieces fall into place, suggesting that the end was contained in the beginning, as it seems to some (mistakenly) that evolution designed the eye to see, the hand to grasp.

But although in human developments, as in natural ones, teleology is generally a delusion, we tend, nevertheless, to act in concert within our groups, as if we were going somewhere. We share something within such groups, and whether we call it religion, nationalism, theory, ideology, or (as Burroughs and biotechnology workers see it) a virus, the effect of these systems is to bind our capacity for enjoyment to a conviction of reality, reason, and purpose. At the same time, these convictions help us to forget that the resulting passions have a perverse origin, one unconcerned with our ends. The undeniable evil (I cannot help but see it as such) done in the name of religion and nation by groups on both sides of the conflict in *Before the Rain* is tied to a human capacity for elemental experiences of hatred and love. The drives represented by these feelings motivate the antagonists' deeds, and the consequences of their actions feed the feelings. And if the actors in this tragedy lament and even condemn the suffering they contribute to, they nevertheless gain access to passions they are reluctant to forgo.

The layers of culture (religion, reason, nationality, etc.) that define much of what it means to be human and that, evidently, protect us from ourselves are always conservative principles, favoring repetition over change, ensuring that the passions find expression in modes that compulsively return us to the same place (which is one of the defining characteristics of the Real) and consequently to the circle. The capacity for enjoyment is systematically redirected from the earliest fixations along a complex branching of symbolic forms. As in an organic tree, like those in my back yard, the character of the tree is expressed less in any specific branch than in the pattern of branching: the range of possible branchings is fixed, though the individual branch is not. Symbolic choice is never random. However, because the original fixations arise from a specific historical scene, a product of accident as well as planning, the conditions for enjoyment that were prepared on that scene contain the seeds of randomness, chance, and contingency – fixation, perversely, provides the swerve that unsettles our expectations and introduces variation. Change can arise, that is, from what is most archaic in human experience, from the work of reaching back into the past and not, as we generally imagine, from our deliberate creation of a future.

Just as Freud imagines that sexuality rises above the pathological when it is turned to the making of children, we imagine ourselves free, transcendent (in Sartre's terms), fully human only when we abjure the temptations of ancient songs and make our own lives. Depending on the particular historical context, the noble man is likely to find women, children, blacks, tropical peoples, slaves, and/ or dogs to be stigmatized by their perverse refusal or inability to rise above their bodies: bound to secret sources of enjoyment, he might say, *those people* are pathological and perverse, while *I* create myself. One's refusal of his own perversity, that is, implies a faith that subjective agency is adequate to explain his actions. The peculiar delights (and horrors) of war, terrorism, torture, and genocide (just to mention a few common expressions of national life that have marked American history) do not contradict the rational ground of that subjective agency so long as those perverse elements are not allowed to become "pathological" but serve a vibrant national health. Just as Freud could overcome his evident distaste for (and fascination with) perverse sexuality by placing it within a productive context of aims and intentions, by making what is fundamentally ungoverned an aspect of design, so we obscure the perverse in our public lives.

Simply to accept the perverse, however, is not a clear alternative. One might wish to recognize that kernel of one's being, the sinthome, the core of enjoyment, but like the Lacanian Real, it necessarily remains inaccessible to the conscious subject, secure against symbolic mastery. And such acceptance certainly would not mean you should follow your heart to whatever realms of pedophilia, coprophagy, or sadism your impulses lead you – not necessarily. Whatever the source of the perverse is, it comes in sublime mystery, whether dressed as Mt. Snowdon or a pair of black patent leather pumps. We are knowers who remain, as Nietzsche comments, unknown to ourselves, which might suggest that we would be wiser to doubt our reasons than trust in either logic or heart. We act because we must, but we need not assume or require that our actions will be the means to ends we have foretold.

The scenes on which we stage our enjoyment have no playwright, only a reader which we call the future. The photographer at the end of *Before the Rain* places his body between two groups knowing he might be shot, but not knowing what effect his death will have. He is shot, and as he dies, he smiles quietly, sublimely. Assume that his smile was not for us, not something to give a local witness or cinematic viewer hope, but a manifestation of his joy, whether inspired by a successfully realized enactment of a fantasy or merely by the rapture of blood loss. In such a case, we would not have to think that the action was intended by the character or director to alter the cycle of death nor to *mean* that now things will be different. But neither should we think that nothing will change.

We, like the actor, cannot know what the effect will be. However, his performance is an affront to the rest who act, who kill, with a heedless certainty that only those possessing moral conviction can display. Such conviction, after all, is generally taken as evidence of subjective authority, the advantage deriving from personal strength or from a commitment to transcendent forces. So appealing is this advantage that those who lack conviction often desire to possess it, or be possessed by it. The extreme, the postmodern version of Foucault's vision of the modern world, sees the subject, by contrast, as a pure production of power. Mark Edmundson, commenting on Don DeLillo's characters, says that unlike those who have appeared in literature from Shakespeare through Freud, DeLillo's lack a full, agonistic self: each is "a conductor, a relay point amid numberless others, for currents of force that are subtly, comprehensively penetrating" (108). Like the lines we tend to draw between the daring hero and the merely (if regrettably) insane, this distinction between a full self and a rigged-up puppet opposes an essential, true being to a constructed or damaged one. But there may be no meaningful choice outside the structures of politics, family, and finances, although there may be a meaningless one. When the photographer acts, he abandons the role provided for him by his ethnic, political script, refusing to depend on the national power for his pleasure, refusing to accept that role as given. In choosing to derive his enjoyment (that sublime smile) from unreasonable sources, he gives up the fantasy that he can control events. He refuses to reinforce a political fixation and embraces a meaningless (for the moment) joy. At best, an altered situation, a break in the circle, may produce the opportunity for some good. But in accepting the fact of his perversity, the link between his capacity for joy and an ancient fixation, he need not cloak the fact in nationalism. And refusing that cloak may be the most important decision in determining how one might enact enjoyment.

NOTES

---

1. Introduction: The Problem with Pleasure

1. Žižek coins the term the "Subject Supposed to Enjoy" by analogy with Lacan's "Subject Supposed to Know." In both cases, an actual person imagines, supposes a Subject to exist who knows or enjoys what the person feels him- or herself to lack. The resentment implied in such supposings nevertheless provides the reassurance that true enjoyment and knowledge are possible: if someone possesses them, then someday I may as well. H. L. Mencken's comment on Puritans' fear that "someone, somewhere may be happy" mirrors Žižek's insight.

2. Jocasta reassures Oedipus as he begins to suspect that he has been married to his mother: "No need this mother-marrying frighten you;/ Many a man has dreamt as much. Such things/ Must be forgotten, if life is to be endured" (52, ll. 980–3).

3. Throughout this book I will be using "enjoyment" as a loose equivalent to the French term *jouissance,* a usage suggested by Slavoj Žižek's writings. I use the term to distinguish an experience of intensity, of a loss of ego control and boundaries (which may be felt as horror or delight), from those "pleasures" of satisfaction, of ego gratification.

4. This reading of the film, and in particular her reading of the Billy Zane character, was first proposed to me by Nina Schwartz in conversation. It would be difficult to overestimate the number of other readings I have stolen from her fertile readings of films and novels during the years I wrote this book.

5. Until he had concluded his project, Descartes needed a "provisional moral code," the first principle of which was "to obey the laws and customs of my country, firmly preserving the religion into which God

161

was good enough to have me instructed from childhood, and governing myself in all other matters according to the most moderate opinions and those furthest from excess, commonly accepted in practice by the most prudent people with whom I should have to live" (45).

6. Lyotard argues that two different forms of narrative inform cultures: the narrative of emancipation and the myth. Like myths, narratives of emancipation "fulfill a legitimating function: they legitimate social and political institutions and practices, forms of legislation, ethics, modes of thought, and symbolics. Yet unlike myths, they ground this legitimacy not in an original 'founding' act, but in a future to be brought about, that is in an Idea to realize" (1993: 50). Both forms of narrative exist in modern cultures, with the result that "there will always be a profound tension between what one ought to be and what one is."

7. Speaking of the difference between the Kantian and Lacanian Thing, Žižek writes, "This lack of the Thing constitutive of 'reality' is . . . in its fundamental dimension, not epistemological [i.e., it is not a problem of perceiving what is certainly real, as it is in Kant's analysis], but rather pertains to the paradoxical logic of desire – the paradox being that this Thing is retroactively produced by the very process of symbolization, i.e., that it emerges in the very gesture of its loss" (1993: 37).

8. Chaos theory notes that nonlinear dynamic systems evolve toward increasingly complex forms, not as an effect of some motivating cause but as an inevitable development of the system in time. For a discussion of complexity, see Nicolis and Prigogine.

9. "In short, there is cause only in something that doesn't work. . . . the Freudian unconscious is situated at that point, where, between cause and that which it affects, there is always something wrong" (1978: 23).

10. "Neither model nor copy, the *chora* precedes and underlies figuration. . . . The *chora* is a modality of significance in which the linguistic sign is not yet articulated as the absence of an object and as the distinction between real and symbolic" (1986: 94).

2. *The Sublime Community*

1. Pat Buchanan's uncompromising populism during the 1996 election campaign, with its rejection of every group that threatens his notion of a unified people – the wealthy, the immigrant, the homosexual – is one mainstream version of this longing.

2. I thank Bruce Levy for this insight into the Nixon–Kennedy debate.

3. Re-Poe Man: Poe's Un-American Sublime

1. "Scriti Politi," an '80s rock group, sang a song about Derrida that began: "I'm in love with Jack De-ree-da,/ Read a page and know I need ta/ Take apart my baby's heart,/ I'm in love, I'm in love." Some textual pleasures can be as intense as the real thing.

2. I refer here to the opening of Foucault's *Discipline and Punish* and to Nietzsche's argument about the relationship between punishment and guilt in *The Genealogy of Morals,* especially "Essay 2," sections XII–XIV (209–15).

3. As a gloss on Usher's fear, I would look at the arousing nature of fear at the heart of Michael Powell's *Peeping Tom.* The look of absolute fear that the photographer is attempting to capture is attained by providing his victims a mirror with which to watch their deaths. It is this look of horror that each time allows him to plunge his sharpened tripod (his third leg) into them. See Kaja Silverman's *The Acoustic Mirror* (32–41) for a brilliant reading of the film.

4. This pun on Us-her was first pointed out to me by Stephen McNally in a class I was teaching at Southern Methodist University in 1983.

5. When Lacan says "La femme n'existe pas," he is referring to the idea that all of woman does not fall under the law of castration, as all of man does (1982: 149–52). Something of woman always falls outside. Slavoj Žižek mentioned at a conference on Lacan at Kent State (May 1990) the remarkable similarity between Hawking's structure of the universe and the feminine side of Lacan's structure of sexuation. It is this similarity that suggests the possibility of a perverse cosmology, one that disavows the law of a totalizing science.

4. "Too Resurgent": Liquidity and Consumption in Henry James

1. James's preface to *What Maisie Knew.* While I was writing this chapter, a controversy-of-the-week TV movie featured a child molester who had been a professor of "LEE-ter-at-shure" at Syracuse, as if to imply that devotees of language will pervert children as readily as syllables.

2. Przybylowicz's optimism seems linked to her misunderstanding the Lacanian categories of the Real and Imaginary as being distinct realms that are confused in the late James: "The Jamesian oeuvre culminates in an expressionistic distortion of time and an eroding boundary between the Imaginary and the Real in which the phenomenological consciousness comes to encompass the whole world" (310). Lacan's

image of the Borromean knot makes it clear that the boundaries always do overlap.

3. For instance, John Carlos Rowe (1984), 107–9. James's notebooks certainly imply such a reading (see January 12, 1887).

4. Jacques Lacan discusses this pattern of return and repetition in psycho-analysis in relation to a missed encounter with some "real" trauma: "Where do we meet this real? For what we have in the discovery of psycho-analysis is an encounter, an essential encounter – an appointment to which we are always called with a real that eludes us" (1978: 53). Aspern's critic spends his life trying to keep an appointment with the author, as if he would find there something to console him.

5. The pervasiveness of water in this story was first made dramatically clear to me in a paper read by Evan Carton at Southern Methodist University in November 1988, since published as "The Anxiety of Effluence."

6. The narrator's discomfort in talking about money appears today in what Baudrillard refers to as the "disappearance of 'liquid' currency, the still too visible symbol of the real excretion (fecalité) of real life ..." (1988: 35). Life and capital produce a surplus, a leftover. The problem with money in the narrator's case is that it associates the divine papers of the poet with the business of living bodies.

7. I am employing here Lacan's famous definition of the signifier as that which "represents the subject for another signifier." Money, perhaps better than language in contemporary culture, works in exactly this way to knit the individual subject into the symbolic cloth of social life.

8. See Brian Rotman's Signifying Nothing for an account of this condition in money, mathematics, and art.

9. Lacan speaks of cause as both a "cause to be sustained" and a "lost cause" (1978: 128). This is because we speak of cause only when "something doesn't work" (23), when we cannot see immediately why some event has occurred. It reflects an attempt to impose a rational order where there is a fundamental gap in knowledge, where something real is missing. The Woman who was Juliana is supposed by the narrator to be such a cause.

10. I think of the homes being rebuilt on the beaches in South Carolina and southern California, where an avowed love of the ocean is mixed with a complaint that the government do something more to restrain its effects.

11. "Abstraction today is no longer that of the map, the double, the mirror or the concept. Simulation is no longer that of a territory, a referential being or a substance. It is the generation by models of a real without

origin or reality: a hyperreal. The territory no longer precedes the map, nor survives it. Henceforth, it is the map that precedes the territory – *precession of simulacra* – it is the map that engenders the territory" (1988: 166).

12. Lears's essay on the "therapeutic roots of consumer culture" makes this point in its disguised form, seeing in consumption a "therapeutic ethos stressing self-realization in this world – an ethos characterized by an almost obsessive concern with psychic and physical health" (4). The illness, however, was "weightlessness": "A dread of unreality, a yearning to experience intense 'real life' in all it forms . . ." (6). This need for intensity, I argue, is precisely what opens us to a cultural perversity.

5. *Alphabetic Pleasures:* The Names

1. I also discuss Kristeva's use of *chora* in Chapter 1. See in particular Note 10.

2. Freud does, however, write of an analogous idea in the "anaclitic" object-choice: "The first autoerotic sexual satisfactions are experienced in connection with vital functions which serve the purpose of self-preservation. The sexual instincts are at the outset attached to the satisfaction of the ego-instincts: only later do they become independent of these, and even then we have an indication of that original attachment in the fact that the persons who are concerned with a child's feeding, care, and protection become his earliest sexual objects" (1914: 87). Kristeva's insight is that these early attachments are linked not only to objects but also to the material rhythms that will linger erotically in the child's developing language.

3. Jean Baudrillard makes the argument in *The Mirror of Production* that this fantasy of productivity is the mirror by which we know ourselves and our ideals (19, 20, & *passim*).

4. Tom LeClair argues that "systems theory" provides a paradigm that explains the self-replicating world of Don DeLillo's work, one in which elements interact within a complex and compulsive dynamic of exchange. See especially the introduction to *In the Loop.*

5. I draw here from Derrida's "Fors," the introduction to Abraham and Torok's *The Wolf Man's Magic Word.* As with the encrypted terms in DeLillo's work, for the Wolf Man, the magic word was a source of intense pleasure that he kept hidden from analytic intervention, preserving its power to produce pleasure. It was encrypted, "Not *within* the crypt (the Self's safe) but *by* the crypt and *in* the Unconscious" (xxvi).

Consequently, every probing of the unconscious by psychoanalysis activated the magic word without its ever being spoken.

6. J. G. Ballard's Empire of the Senses: Perversion and the Failure of Authority

1. The patient dreamed, "[h]is father was alive once more and was talking to him in his usual way, but . . . he had really died, only he did not know it" (1900: 430).

2. In his earlier *Hello America*, an America of the twenty-second century, devastated by ecological failure, is being led to recovery by President Charles Manson, a madman who took his name from the twentieth-century pied piper. Reviewing Norman Mailer's *The Executioner's Song*, Ballard notes the fame Manson achieved, the peculiar way this psychopath "expanded to fill the roles assigned to him" by American culture, and speculates that Lee Harvey Oswald, had he survived, would be a free man and a TV celebrity. (This review, "Killing Time Should Be Prime Time TV," and many other reviews, stories, interviews, and bibliographies have been collected in *Re/Search: J. G. Ballard*.)

3. The effect of constant observation is to destroy the internal symbolic world that allows most adults to think and act with some sense of individual responsibility. The distress suffered by the four women imprisoned in the federal detention center in Lexington, Kentucky, fully panoptic in its structure, is proof of the trauma that such a facility can produce. They experienced both physical and psychic damage (Norman and Reuben).

4. Lacan argues that love has a destructive element to it because it always reaches for something beyond the beloved. The lover says, "I love you, but because inexplicably I love in you something more than you – the *objet petit a* – I mutilate you." The image is of a lover taking the beloved to pieces looking for the object – a breast, an eye, a mouth – that will explain the love. At the same time, the lover feels unworthy of the sought-for love and so says: "I give myself to you, . . . but this gift of my person – as they say – Oh, mystery! is changed inexplicably into a gift of shit" (1978: 268). No part taken by the beloved will survive loving consumption without being transformed in the end.

5. Baudrillard sees the real in the contemporary world to be "that for which it is possible to provide an equivalent representation," a claim that is justified by most practices of science, journalism, and law. But as habit naturalizes these practices, "the real becomes not only that which

can be reproduced, but that which is always already reproduced: the hyperreal." Television producers' attempts to show real cops on duty seem unable to escape the imagery of the fictions that came first, with the effect, as Baudrillard comments, that an "air of nondeliberate parody clings to everything." Death loses its seriousness in such a context (1988: 145–6).

6. Such an inversion of what was once considered interior life occurs in the work of Dali, Magritte, and Ernst, artists Ballard admires. In their images, the obsessions that shape desire take the form of mundane objects – a hat, a leg – wrenched from the sensible surroundings. A surrealist painter, Ballard comments, shows things in "a glossy isolation, as if all the objects in its landscape had been drained of their emotional association, the accretions of sentiment and common usage" (1984: 103).

7. The question of whether this limited willingness to understand is Ballard's or the character's is undecidable: at what level does the unspeakable emerge? My point in discussing a number of Ballard's books is to show the transformations that occur throughout his career as he returns to the trauma of childhood violence. In his novel-autobiography, *The Kindness of Women,* Jamie's story begins with the war and prison camp of *The Empire of the Sun,* but unlike Jim in the earlier book, Jamie feels little of the ecstatic horror, and he has a companion, a girl who remains a friend into his adulthood. Ballard has, it seems, put an earlier vision of his experience behind him, but only by forgoing the understanding of perverse enjoyment that informed his earlier work.

8. Compare Caserio's sense of the efficacy of perversion with that of Janine Chasseguet-Smirgel: "perversion represents a . . . reconstitution of chaos, out of which there arises a new kind of reality, that of the anal universe. This will take the place of the psycho-sexual genital dimension, that of the Father" (11). She sees no compulsion in the perverse subject to rejoin the Father's world.

9. Lacan writes, "The primal repressed is a signifier" (1978: 176), a proposition that distinguishes him from those who imagine that what is repressed is reality. Only when we forget that the first representation of our love – Mother's face – was a signifier (i.e., not Mother herself) is the fantasy of the Mother locked into place.

10. Caserio and Emerson comment at length on this aspect of the story, an indication of how disturbing they find it.

7. Fatal West: W. S. Burroughs's Perverse Destiny

1. Frederick Dolan convincingly demolishes any hope that Burroughs would lead us out of the wilderness, demonstrating how clearly Burroughs remains within a Romantic metaphysics.

2. See for example "Women's Time," 187–213. Kristeva argues that a rejection of the symbolic is "lived as the rejection of the paternal function and ultimately generat[es] psychoses" (199), but by the end of even this early essay, she is proposing the highly suspect category of "guiltless maternity" (206) as a way of evading the impasse of the law. If there is a solution to the problem of patriarchy here, she does not find it through the Aristotelian construct.

3. For a discussion of sinthome, see the discussion in Chapter 1.

4. "Stoicism" is a position Hegel describes dialectically, wherein one has moved beyond a slavish belief in authority but has achieved freedom by becoming "*indifferent* to natural existence . . . , lacking the fullness of life" (122). For Lacan, this faith in the power of the individual mind, the cogito, to think itself to the truth becomes the delusion of those whose faith in the "name of the father," the "*nom du père*," displays how the "non-duped err." The cynical reasoner accepts the contradictions implicit in his position and yet continues to assert its validity.

5. See Žižek, 1989: 29–33. Žižek develops this formulation out of Peter Sloterdijk's book *Critique of Cynical Reason* (1983).

6. Chomsky recounts St. Augustine's story of a pirate, putting it in the context of international terrorism by the democratic Western nations:

[A] pirate [was] captured by Alexander the Great, who asked him "how he dares molest the sea." "How dare you molest the whole world?" the pirate replied: "because I do it with a little ship only, I am called a thief; you, doing it with a great navy, are called an Emperor." (1)

7. For a good summary of the relation of fantasy to sexuality, see Teresa de Lauretis, 81–5.

8. Philip Kuberski's "Hardcopy" has developed the metaphor of viral information in the late twentieth century to speculate on the relation between computers, ideology, and subjectivity. Commenting on the film *Blade Runner,* he notes the murderous rage of one replicant who destroys his creator:

This scene dramatizes the film's major concern: what precisely does a man do when he learns, as has postmodern man, that his subjectivity is an artefact of society, and that his body is the accidental product of mutation and the manifestation, like a computer or a television, of Information. (70)

The dilemma is that this man, constituted of information, should be both superior to "natural" men and yet inhumanly, abjectly inferior.

9. Lacan introduces the "lamella" to identify "the relation between the living subject and that which he loses by having to pass, for his repro-duction, through the sexual cycle" (1978: 199). Sexual reproduction means that there is something in us that is not us, that is unconcerned with the fate of the individual subject. The mortal subject lives with the undead of replication.

10. Compare with Wallace Stevens's "Snowman," who "nothing himself, beholds/ Nothing that is not there, and the nothing that is." See also Brian Rotman's brilliant analysis of nothing, *Signifying Nothing: The Semiotics of Zero*. In this book, he traces various ways in which *nothing* has served both a productive and disturbing function in the Western world.

11. The interpretations other Cities of the Red Night gave to the words are:

The city of partisans: "Here, everything is as true as you think it is and everything you can get away with is permitted."
The university city: "Complete permission derives from complete un-derstanding."
The cities of illusion: "Nothing is true and *therefore* everything is per-mitted." (158–9)

12. This is an idea I develop in Chapter 5.

13. See "Introduction" (this volume).

14. The "cut-in" or "cut-up" in Burroughs's own work and in that of his character Clem Snide involves assembling information (taped sounds, news clippings, etc.) cut at random from some source. Burroughs describes it:

The cut-up method brings to writers the collage, which has been used by painters for fifty years. And used by the moving and still camera. In fact all street shots from movie or still cameras are by the unpre-dictable factors of passersby and juxtaposition cut-ups. And photogra-phers will tell you that often their best shots are accidents . . . writers will tell you the same. The best writing seems to be done almost by accident but writers until the cut-up method was made explicit – all writing is in fact cut-ups . . . – had no way to produce the accident of spontaneity. You cannot *will* spontaneity. But you can introduce the unpredictable spontaneous factor with a pair of scissors. (1982: 35)

8. Conclusion: Agency in the Perverse

1. Jonathan Dollimore's development of the "perverse dynamic" adds greatly to the paradox of identity and difference I am discussing in this section. I will not attempt to summarize his subtle argument but refer the reader to *Sexual Dissidence,* particularly to pages 229–30.

BIBLIOGRAPHY

Abraham, Nicolas, and Maria Torok. *The Wolf Man's Magic Word: A Crypto-nymy.* Trans. Nicholas Rand. Minneapolis: U of Minnesota P, 1986.

The Adjuster. Dir. Atom Egoyan. Orion, 1992.

Agnew, Jean-Christophe. "The Consuming Vision of Henry James." In Richard Wrightman Fox and T. J. Jackson Lears, eds., *The Culture of Consumption: Critical Essays in American History, 1880–1980* (New York: Pantheon, 1983), 65–100.

Arendt, Hannah. *On Revolution.* New York: Viking, 1963.

Ballard, J. G. *The Atrocity Exhibition.* 1970. San Francisco: Re/Search, 1990.

    Crash. 1973. New York: Vintage, 1985.

    Empire of the Sun. New York: Pocket–Simon, 1985.

    Hello America. London: Jonathan Cape, 1981.

    "Killing Time Should Be Prime Time TV." *The Guardian,* Nov. 15, 1979. Rpt. in *Re/Search: J. G. Ballard,* 108–9.

    The Kindness of Women. New York: Farrar, 1991.

    Re/Search: J. G. Ballard. San Francisco: Re/Search, 1984.

    Running Wild. New York: Farrar, 1989.

Barthelme, Donald. *The Dead Father.* 1975. New York: Penguin, 1986.

Baudrillard, Jean. *The Mirror of Production.* Trans. Mark Poster. St. Louis: Telos Press, 1975.

    Selected Writings. Ed. Mark Poster. Stanford, Calif.: Stanford UP, 1988.

Benjamin, Walter. "Paris, Capital of the Nineteenth Century." In Edmund Jephcott, trans., *Reflections.* New York: Harcourt, 1978.

Bloom, Harold. *The American Religion: The Emergence of the Post-Christian Nation.* New York: Simon, 1992.

Burroughs, William S. *Cities of the Red Night.* New York: Holt, 1981.

    Re/Search: William S. Burroughs, Brion Gysin, Throbbing Gristle. San Francisco: Re/Search, 1982.

171

The Western Lands. New York: Penguin, 1987.

Butler, Judith. *Gender Trouble: Feminism and the Subversion of Identity.* New York: Routledge, 1990.

Calasso, Roberto. *The Ruin of Kasch.* Trans. William Weaver and Stephen Sartarelli. Cambridge, Mass.: Belknap P of Harvard UP, 1994.

Carton, Evan. "The Anxiety of Effluence: Criticism, Currency, and *The Aspern Papers.*" *HJR* 10 (1989): 135–141.

Caserio, Robert L. "Mobility and Masochism: Christine Brooke-Rose and J. G. Ballard." *Novel: A Forum on Fiction* 21 (1988): 292–310.

Chasseguet-Smirgel, Janine. *Creativity and Perversion.* New York: Norton, 1984.

Chomsky, Noam. *Pirates and Emperors: International Terrorism in the Real World.* New York: Claremont, 1986.

Churchland, Patricia Smith. *Neurophilosophy: Toward a Unified Science of the Mind/Brain.* Cambridge, Mass.: MIT P, 1986.

Clavreul, Jean. "The Perverse Couple." In Stuart Schneiderman, ed. and trans., *Returning to Freud: Clinical Psychoanalysis in the School of Lacan.* New Haven, Conn.: Yale UP, 1980.

Connor, Steven. *Theory and Cultural Value.* Oxford: Blackwell, 1992.

Deleuze, Gilles, and Félix Guatarri. *Anti-Oedipus: Capitalism and Schizophrenia.* Trans. Robert Hurley, Mark Seem, Helen R. Lane. Minneapolis: U of Minnesota P, 1977.

DeLillo, Don. *The Names.* New York: Vintage–Random, 1982.

Mao II. New York: Viking, 1991.

Dennett, Daniel C. *Consciousness Explained.* Boston: Little, 1991.

Derrida, Jacques. "Fors." Foreword to Nicolas Abraham and Maria Torok, *The Wolf Man's Magic Word: A Cryptonymy.* Trans. Nicholas Rand. Minneapolis: U of Minnesota P, 1986.

Descartes, René. *Discourse on Method.* Trans. F. E. Sutcliffe. New York: Penguin, 1968.

Desser, David. *Eros Plus Massacre: An Introduction to the Japanese New Wave Cinema.* Bloomington: Indiana U.P., 1988.

Dolan, Frederick. *Allegories of America: Narratives, Metaphysics, Politics.* Ithaca, N.Y.: Cornell UP, 1994.

"The Poetics of Postmodern Subversion: The Politics of Writing in William S. Burroughs's *The Western Lands.*" *Contemporary Literature* 32 (1991): 534–51.

Dollimore, Jonathan. *Sexual Dissidence: Augustine to Wilde, Freud to Foucault.* Oxford: Oxford UP, 1991.

Drugstore Cowboy. Dir. Gus Van Sant. Avenue Pictures, 1989.

Eagleton, Terry. *Literary Theory: An Introduction*. Minneapolis: U of Minnesota P, 1983.

Edmundson, Mark. "Not Flat, Not Round, Not There: Don DeLillo's Novel Characters." *The Yale Review* 83.2 (1995): 106–24.

Emerson, Gloria. "The Children of the Field." *TriQuarterly* 65 (1986): 226–8.

Emerson, Ralph Waldo. *Selections from Ralph Waldo Emerson*. Ed. Stephen E. Whicher. Boston: Houghton, 1957.

Ewen, Stuart. *Captains of Consciousness: Advertising and the Social Roots of the Consumer Culture*. New York: McGraw, 1976.

Fawcett, Brian. *Public Eye: An Investigation into the Disappearance of the World*. Toronto: HarperCollins, 1990.

Foucault, Michel. *The History of Sexuality, Vol. 1: An Introduction*. 1976. Trans. Robert Hurley. New York: Vintage–Random, 1980.

Discipline and Punish: The Birth of the Prison, 1975. Trans. Alan Sheridan. New York: Vintage–Random, 1979.

Fox, Richard Wrightman, and T. J. Jackson Lears, eds. *The Culture of Consumption: Critical Essays in American History, 1880–1980*. New York: Pantheon, 1983.

Freud, Sigmund. "On Narcissism: An Introduction." 1914. *The Standard Edition of the Complete Psychological Works of Sigmund Freud*. Ed. and trans. James Strachey. Vol. 14: 67–102. London: Hogarth, 1953. 24 vols.

Beyond the Pleasure Principle. 1920. *The Standard Edition of the Complete Psychological Works of Sigmund Freud*. Ed. and trans. James Strachey. Vol. 18: 3–64. London: Hogarth, 1953. 24 vols.

The Interpretation of Dreams. 1900. *The Standard Edition of the Complete Psychological Works of Sigmund Freud*. Ed. and trans. James Strachey. Vols. 4 and 5. London: Hogarth, 1953. Vol. 4: 1–338; vol. 5: 339–627. 24 vols.

Three Essays on the Theory of Sexuality. 1905. *The Standard Edition of the Complete Psychological Works of Sigmund Freud*. Ed. and Trans. James Strachey. Vol. 7: 125–248. London: Hogarth, 1953. 24 vols.

Gallop, Jane. *The Daughter's Seduction: Feminism and Psychoanalysis*. Ithaca, N.Y.: Cornell UP, 1982.

Greenland, Colin. *The Entropy Exhibition: Michael Moorcock and the British "New Wave" in Science Fiction*. London: RKP, 1983.

Greenslade, William. "The Power of Advertising: Chad Newsome and the Meaning of Paris in *The Ambassadors*." *ELH* 49.1 (1982): 99–122.

Gregory, Robert. "The Diddle in the *Purloined Letter.*" *Works and Days* 2 (1985): 49–56.

Hawking, Stephen W. *A Brief History of Time: From the Big Bang to Black Holes.* New York: Bantam, 1988.

Hegel, G. W. F. *Phenomenology of Spirit.* Trans. A. V. Miller. New York: Oxford UP, 1977.

In the Realm of the Senses. Dir. Nagasi Oshima. Surrogate, 1976.

Irwin, John T. *American Hieroglyphics: The Symbol of the Egyptian Hieroglyphics in the American Renaissance.* New Haven, Conn.: Yale UP, 1980.

   The Mystery to a Solution: Poe, Borges, and the Analytic Detective Story. Baltimore: Johns Hopkins UP, 1994.

James, Henry. *The Ambassadors.* New York: Norton, 1964.

   "The Aspern Papers" in *The Turn of the Screw and Other Short Novels.* New York: NAL, 1962.

Kant, Immanuel. *The Critique of Judgement.* Trans. J. H. Bernard. London: Macmillan, 1914.

Kaston, Carren. *Imagination and Desire in the Novels of Henry James.* New Brunswick, N.J.: Rutgers UP, 1985.

Kristeva, Julia. "Revolution in Poetic Language." *The Kristeva Reader.* Trans. Margaret Waller. New York: Columbia UP, 1986, 89–136.

   "Women's Time." Trans. Alice Jardine and Harry Blake. *The Kristeva Reader.* Ed. Toril Moi. New York: Columbia UP, 1986, 187–213.

   Black Sun: Depression and Melancholia. Trans. Leon S. Roudiez. New York: Columbia UP, 1989.

   Powers of Horror: An Essay on Abjection. Trans. Leon S. Roudiez. New York: Columbia UP, 1982.

Kuberski, Philip F. "Hardcopy: The Remains of the Cold War." *Arizona Quarterly: A Journal of American Literature, Culture, and Theory.* 46.2 (1990): 55–71.

   The Persistence of Memory. Berkeley: U of California P, 1992.

Kulowski, Jacob. *Crash Injuries: The Integrated Medical Aspects of Automobile Injuries and Deaths.* Springfield, Ill.: Charles C Thomas, 1960.

Lacan, Jacques. "Seminar on 'The Purloined Letter.'" *YFS* 48 (1972) 39–72.

   Ecrits: A Selection. Trans. Alan Sheridan. New York: Norton, 1977.

   Feminine Sexuality: Jacques Lacan and the "école freudienne." Trans. Jacqueline Rose. New York: Norton, 1982.

   The Four Fundamental Concepts of Psychoanalysis, 1973. Trans. Alan Sheridan. Ed. Jacques-Alain Miller. New York: Norton, 1978.

Lauretis, Teresa de. *The Practice of Love: Lesbian Sexuality and Perverse Desire.* Bloomington: Indiana UP, 1994.

Lears, T. J. Jackson. "From Salvation to Self-Realization: Advertising and the Therapeutic Roots of the Consumer Culture, 1880–1930." In Richard Wrightman Fox and T. J. Jackson Lears, eds., *The Culture of Consumption: Critical Essays in American History, 1880–1980* (New York: Pantheon, 1983), 1–38.

LeClair, Tom. *In the Loop: Don DeLillo and the Systems Novel.* Urbana: U of Illinois P, 1987.

Lyotard, Jean-François. *The Inhuman: Reflections on Time.* Trans. Geoffrey Bennington and Rachel Bowlby. Stanford, Calif.: Stanford UP, 1991.

   The Postmodern Explained. Trans. and Ed. Julian Pefanis and Morgan Thomas. Minneapolis: U of Minnesota P, 1993.

   The Postmodern Condition: A Report on Knowledge. Trans. Geoffrey Bennington and Brian Massumi. Minneapolis: U of Minnesota P, 1984.

MacLean, Paul D. "Brain Evolution Relating to Family, Play, and the Separation Call." *Archives of General Psychiatry* 42, 1985: 405–417.

Marcus, James. Rev. of *Running Wild*, by J. G. Ballard. *The New York Times Book Review* 17 Dec. 1989: 19.

Marcuse, Herbert. *One Dimensional Man: Studies in the Ideology of Advanced Industrial Society.* London: Routledge, 1964.

Maves, Carl. *Sensuous Pessimism: Italy in the Work of Henry James.* Bloomington: Indiana UP, 1973.

Miles, Barry. *William Burroughs: el hombre invisible.* New York: Hyperion, 1992.

Morgan, Marabel. *The Total Woman.* New York: Pocket–Simon, 1973.

Nancy, Jean-Luc. *The Inoperative Community.* Ed. Peter Connor. Trans. Peter Connor, Lisa Garbus, Michael Holland, Simona Sawhney. Minneapolis: U of Minnesota P, 1991.

Nicolis, Grégoire, and Ilya Prigogine. *Exploring Complexity: An Introduction.* New York: Freeman, 1989.

Nietzsche, Friedrich. *The Birth of Tragedy* and *The Genealogy of Morals.* Trans. Francis Golffing. Garden City, N.Y.: Doubleday, 1956.

Norman, Carlos, and William A. Reuben. *The Nation* 27 June 1987: 881+.

P.M. *Bolo'Bolo.* New York: Semiotext(e), 1985.

Paris Is Burning. Dir. Jennie Livingston. Academy Entertainment, 1992.

Poe, Edgar Allan. *Poetry and Tales.* New York: The Library of America, 1984.

Przybylowicz, Donna. *Desire and repression: the dialectic of self and other in the late works of Henry James.* Tuscaloosa: U of Alabama P, 1986.

Rorty, Richard. "Philosophy as a Kind of Writing: An Essay on Derrida." *Consequences of Pragmatism: (Essays: 1972–1980).* Minneapolis: U of Minnesota P, 1982.

Rotman, Brian. *Signifying Nothing: The Semiotics of Zero.* Stanford, Calif.: Stanford UP, 1987.

Rowe, John Carlos. *The Theoretical Dimensions of Henry James.* Madison: Wisconsin UP, 1984.

    Through the Custom House: Nineteenth-Century Fiction and Modern Theory. Baltimore: Johns Hopkins UP, 1982.

Samuels, Robert. "How Come?" From an unpublished typescript.

San Francisco Chronicle 29 Dec. 1991, A1.

Sante, Luc. "Tales from the Dark Side." *The New York Times Magazine* 9 Sept. 1990: 58+.

Sedgwick, Eve Kosofsky. "The Beast in the Closet: James and the Writing of Homosexual Panic." In Ruth Bernard Yeazell, ed., *Sex, Politics and Science in the Nineteenth-Century Novel.* Baltimore: Johns Hopkins UP, 1986.

Seitz, Don Carlos. *Under the Black Flag.* New York: The Dial Press, 1925.

Shell, Marc. "The Gold Bug." *Genre* 13 (1980), 11–30.

Silverman, Kaja. *The Acoustic Mirror: The Female Voice in Psychoanalysis and Cinema.* Bloomington and Indianapolis: Indiana UP, 1988.

Sloterdijk, Peter. *Critique of Cynical Reason.* Minneapolis: U of Minnesota P, 1987.

Sophocles. *King Oedipus.* Trans. E. F. Watling. Baltimore: Penguin, 1947.

Stanley, Eric. "Influence, Commerce, and the Literary Magazine." *The Missouri Review* 8 (1985): 177–93.

Tanner, Tony. "Proust, Ruskin, and James and *Le Desire de Venise.*" *Journal of American Studies* 21 (1987): 5–29.

Vaughn, Larry. "Poe and the Mystery of Things: A Remembrance." *Substance* 42 13 (1983): 95–98.

Žižek, Slavoj. *Looking Awry: An Introduction to Jacques Lacan through Popular Culture.* Cambridge, Mass.: MIT P, 1991.

    The Sublime Object of Ideology. New York: Verso, 1989.

    Tarrying with the Negative: Kant, Hegel, and the Critique of Ideology. Durham, N.C.: Duke UP, 1993.

INDEX

177

The following titles are out of print: